The Battle for the Court

Constitutionalism and Democracy

GREGG IVERS AND
KEVIN T. MCGUIRE,
EDITORS

The Battle for the Court

INTEREST GROUPS, JUDICIAL ELECTIONS, AND PUBLIC POLICY

Lawrence Baum,
David Klein,
and Matthew J. Streb

UNIVERSITY OF VIRGINIA PRESS CHARLOTTESVILLE AND LONDON

University of Virginia Press

Printed in the United States of America on acid-free paper

First published 2017

9 8 7 6 5 4 3 2 1

Library of Congress Cataloging-in-Publication Data

Names: Baum, Lawrence, author. | Klein, David E., 1970– author. | Streb, Matthew J. (Matthew Justin), 1974–, author.
Title: The battle for the court : interest groups, judicial elections, and public policy / Lawrence Baum, David Klein, and Matthew J. Streb.
Description: Charlottesville, VA : University of Virginia Press, 2017. | Series: Constitutionalism and democracy | Includes bibliographical references and index.
Identifiers: LCCN 2017010444 | ISBN 9780813940342 (cloth : alk. paper) | ISBN 9780813940359 (ebook)
Subjects: LCSH: Judges—United States—Election. | Judges—Selection and appointment—United States. |Political questions and judicial power—United States.
Classification: LCC KF8776 .B38 2017 | DDC 347.73/314—dc23
LC record available at https://lccn.loc.gov/2017010444

[The $500,000 cap on non-economic compensatory damages in] section 2-1115.1 disregards the jury's careful deliberative process in determining damages that will fairly compensate injured plaintiffs who have proven their causes of action. . . . Therefore, section 2-1115.1 unduly encroaches upon the fundamentally judicial prerogative of determining whether a jury's assessment of damages is excessive within the meaning of the law.
—Illinois Supreme Court (*Best v. Taylor Machine Works*, 689 N.E.2d 1057, 1080 [1997])

For too long, the plaintiff's bar had the field to itself as far as judicial selections. Now, business interests and tort reform groups have come together to get engaged in the political arena and worked to inform the public about judicial selections.
—Sherman Joyce, President, American Tort Reform Association (quoted in Clifton Barnes, "Tort Reform Momentum Slowed but Not Stopped" [2005])

Dude, we need tort reform.
—Frequent refrain of Mike Piazza, catcher for the New York Mets (quoted in David Waldstein, "A Star Who Gave the Mets a Jolt, and Not Just at the Plate" [2016])

CONTENTS

FIGURES AND TABLES

ACKNOWLEDGMENTS

We are deeply indebted to many people whose work helped make this book possible and whose feedback was invaluable. The analysis of voting decisions by individual Ohioans in chapter 3 was possible because of the work of a great many people on the series of election-related surveys conducted in the Department of Political Science at Ohio State University over the years. Especially important were the two department faculty members who initiated, sustained, and supervised the surveys, Herbert Weisberg and Aage Clausen. The political science department and the College of Social and Behavioral Sciences at Ohio State provided funding for the surveys over the years, and the National Science Foundation provided funding for the extensive 1990 surveys.

In working with the Ohio election data over the years, we have received good advice and assistance from many scholars, whom we have thanked in prior publications. We are especially grateful to Marie Hojnacki and Emily Rock, who were coauthors with one of us on articles about Ohio Supreme Court elections and whose ideas are reflected in what we have written in this book.

In developing and carrying out this project, we learned a great deal from the ideas and research of the small but thriving scholarly community that studies elections to state supreme courts. Especially helpful in these respects were Chris Bonneau, Damon Cann, Jim Gibson, Melinda Gann Hall, and Bert Kritzer. We owe a similar debt to Kathleen Barber, Mary Cornelia Porter, and Alan Tarr for their pioneering work on the Ohio Supreme Court.

We relied heavily on the publications, records, and website of the

Secretary of State's office in Ohio for data on voting patterns and on campaign expenditures. Rose Ferguson of the Secretary of State's office was especially helpful in locating expenditure records from elections in the distant past. The Center for Responsive Politics, through its website OpenSecrets.org, provided data on amounts and sources of financial contributions to state supreme court candidates. We appreciate the help of Sarah Bryner, CRP Research Director, in interpreting these data. We benefited from the data on voting in state supreme court elections that Bert Kritzer has compiled and made available at his website. We also benefited from the research assistance provided by Aaron Kushner.

The anonymous reviewers for the University of Virginia Press provided us with valuable suggestions for development of our manuscript and for revision of that manuscript. We appreciate their insights. We also appreciate the support of Gregg Ivers and Kevin McGuire, editors of the Constitutionalism and Democracy series for the Press. Morgan Myers, Mark Mones, and Siobhan Drummond provided a great deal of help in turning the manuscript into a book.

Dick Holway, editor for History and Social Sciences at the Press, played an essential role in this project. Throughout our work on the book, he provided both encouragement and excellent advice. We were (and are) very fortunate to work with him.

The Battle for the Court

INTRODUCTION

State Farm had a problem. In 1997, the insurance company had suffered a substantial loss in a class action lawsuit that accused the company of breaching its contract with policyholders by using aftermarket parts, rather than parts from the original manufacturer, to repair the cars it insured. A jury and judge combined to award some State Farm policyholders more than $1 billion. After the verdict was affirmed on appeal, State Farm petitioned the Illinois Supreme Court to hear the case. The state supreme court heard oral arguments in May 2003 but still had not reached a decision when Justice Philip Rarick announced that he would not seek reelection in November 2004. The candidates running for the seat that Rarick was vacating were two sitting lower-court judges, Republican Lloyd Karmeier and Democrat Gordon Maag.

State Farm saw its chance, realizing that the winner of the contest for Rarick's seat in Illinois's Fifth District would have significant influence on the outcome of the appealed case.[1] The insurance giant donated $350,000 to Karmeier's campaign.[2] State Farm was not the only organization to take an active interest in the contest. Karmeier raised $4.8 million altogether, with most of his money coming from the Illinois Republican Party, business associations, health professionals, and insurance. His opponent Maag raised $4.5 million, almost all of which came from the Illinois Democratic Party and Justice for All, a political action committee supported primarily by attorneys who represent individual plaintiffs in civil cases (commonly referred to as "trial lawyers") and by labor organizations. Although the political parties contributed the lion's share of money to the candidates, most of the money they raised came from the interest groups supporting the candidates (Goldberg et al. 2005, 17–19).

The campaigns looked something like what one might expect from candidates for the United States Congress. Maag, the Democratic Party, and Justice for All PAC accused Karmeier of being in cahoots with groups like State Farm who were trying to unduly influence the court and hurt the middle class. One Justice for All commercial depicted recently laid-off mine workers saying that "Karmeier is in the pocket of big business" and "Maag is going to be for the working man."[3] Karmeier, the Republican Party, and JUSTPAC (the political action committee of the Illinois Civil Justice League) argued that Maag was beholden to trial lawyers and engaged in backroom politics. Several ads accused Maag of contributing to a health care "crisis" because of frivolous lawsuits related to medical malpractice.

The race was about more than just the influence of organized interests on the candidates. Both candidates were accused by groups supporting the other candidate of being soft on crime. Notably, the groups that sponsored the crime-related attack ads were not victims' rights groups or law enforcement agencies, but political parties or other groups that had more of an interest in civil cases than in criminal justice. Take this one anti-Karmeier ad:

> He used candy to lure the children into the house. Once inside, the three children were sexually molested. A four-year-old girl raped. Her brothers sodomized. A Belleville man was arrested and convicted for the crime after trying to develop pictures of the abuse. Despite the prosecutor's objections Judge Lloyd Karmeier gave him probation, saying, "The court should grant leniency . . ." Another case where Karmeier let a violent criminal out into the community. Lloyd Karmeier—the wrong choice for supreme court.

The ad was sponsored by the Democratic Party, which, along with Justice for All, accused Karmeier of giving only probation to kidnappers who murdered a 92-year-old grandmother and of reducing bail for a couple who beat their child to death. The Republican Party and JUSTPAC struck back, highlighting Maag's votes to overturn the convictions of a man who sexually assaulted a six-year-old girl and a man who planned to kill his girlfriend.

The election went as State Farm hoped. Karmeier won, carrying 55 percent of the vote. He then chose not to recuse himself from the State

Farm case, though he was under pressure to do so because of the company's financial support of his campaign, and was part of a 4-2 majority that voted to overturn the $1.1 billion verdict.[4]

Although attention had been focused on State Farm's stakes in the case, other companies and interest groups recognized that the case had potential implications reaching far beyond the specific parties. The court received nineteen amicus curiae briefs from Allstate Insurance Company, the National Association of Independent Insurers, the American Insurance Association, the Alliance of American Insurers, the Chamber of Commerce of the United States, General Motors, Public Citizen, and Trial Lawyers for Public Justice, among others. Although the opinion of the court emphasized factual specifics, it also touched on larger legal issues of class certification and contract interpretation and sent clear signals about the prospects for success of similar lawsuits in the future. The dissenting justices read the opinion as a heavy-handed attempt to discourage class action litigation. Corporate counsel reporting on the decision in an industry periodical agreed about the probable impact: "The *Avery* decision is likely to substantially curb (and perhaps entirely eliminate) efforts by the plaintiff's bar to attack the specification of [aftermarket] parts through the class action process. In addition, the decision may further discourage the plaintiff's bar from pursuing national class action litigation based upon insurance claims handling practices" (Nelson, Cohen, and Rosenberg 2005, 9).

The Karmeier-Maag contest is hardly typical of state supreme court elections in its scope and tone, but it illustrates the development of "new-style" judicial elections. As early as the mid-1980s, law professor Roy Schotland (1985, 76) concluded that judicial campaigns had become "noisier, nastier, and costlier." That trend has continued in the three decades since then. There are still many supreme court contests that are small in scale and genteel in tone, and there are states in which judicial elections have changed little. But well-funded and sharp-edged campaigns in which interest groups take an active role have become increasingly common.

Several characteristics are common to most high-profile supreme court races in which interest groups are engaged. Business groups representing such industries as health or insurance line up on one side, trial lawyers and labor on the other. The groups on both sides are motivated primarily by issues in tort law concerning compensation for personal injuries and related matters such as property damage. Business groups seek to change the law to limit their liability for damages in tort law, often under the general banner of "tort reform"; groups on the other side oppose such changes. However, the public campaigns often focus on crime or candidate qualifications rather than, for instance, caps on medical malpractice lawsuits or interpretations of uninsured motorist provisions in auto insurance policies. Occasionally other issues drive large-scale campaigns, as same-sex marriage did in the retention elections for three Iowa Supreme Court justices in 2010 (see May 2013, 61–64), but most of the time it is economic issues—and especially torts—that spur large-scale campaigns.

New-style electoral contests for judgeships have received a great deal of attention from people who are interested in state courts, including scholars. That attention has focused on campaigns themselves, their impact on the vote and on citizens' attitudes toward the courts, and their implications for systems used to elect judges.[5] This is understandable, as these are all important matters.

They are not the only important matters, though, and the single most important matter has received the least attention of all. The policies of state supreme courts can have an enormous impact on the fortunes of groups such as labor and the business community and on the lives of people in a state. Interest groups involve themselves in campaigns for seats on state supreme courts because they recognize this fact and care a great deal about the policies that those courts make. Although scholars have given considerable attention to the impact of elections as an institution on judges' policy choices, there has been little examination of the relationship between changes in supreme court elections and the policies that supreme courts make.[6]

In this book we focus on those policy stakes. We examine how supreme court policies have spurred activity by interest groups and others that make new-style contests possible, how campaign activity and the outcomes of elections affect court policies, and how voters serve as a link between group activities and court policies. We undertake those inquiries through a close examination of campaigns, voting, and court policies on torts in Ohio over a period of more than three decades.

We set the stage for these inquiries in this introduction. First, we discuss the evolution of judicial elections. Second, we briefly examine the burgeoning research on judicial elections and how our inquiry relates to that body of scholarship. Third, we make a case for focusing on tort reform battles in a single state (Ohio) and provide background information on what happened in Ohio. Finally, we lay out the structure of the book and how we will proceed.

The Evolution of Judicial Elections

Although judicial elections have seeped into the public's consciousness only recently, the idea of electing judges is hardly new.[7] The thirteen original states all employed an appointment system at first; some had the governor appoint judges while others had the state legislature appoint. But early in their histories, Vermont, Indiana, and Georgia all made some use of judicial elections for their lower courts. In 1832 Mississippi became the first state to amend its constitution to require that all state judges be elected. After Mississippi changed, the popularity of elected state judiciaries grew. Every state that entered the Union from 1846 until Alaska's admission in 1959 allowed for the election of some, if not all, of its judges. Even some of the original states, including New York, eventually opted for elections as the selection method for at least some of their judges.

The states that initially adopted elections as means to select judges used a partisan ballot for judicial contests. By the late nineteenth century, distrust of parties led to a widespread movement for nonpartisan elections. From the early twentieth century on, this movement enjoyed considerable success. As a result, a substantial majority of the states that elect some or all of their judges today use nonpartisan elections.

In the early twentieth century, reformers associated with the Progressive movement developed an alternative system that has been labeled the Missouri Plan or merit selection, in which commissions nominate candidates for judgeships, the governor chooses from the nominees, and the voters periodically vote yes or no on a new term for a sitting judge in retention elections (American Judicature Society 2011). This system has been widely adopted by states, either for all of their courts or for appellate courts.

As of 2016, seven states choose supreme court justices through partisan elections, though three of those states (Illinois, New Mexico, and Pennsylvania) use retention elections after a justice's first election. Fifteen states use nonpartisan elections. Fifteen states use the Missouri Plan. In the remaining thirteen states, the governor or legislature selects justices; in one of those states (California), gubernatorial appointees run for additional terms in retention elections. In three states with gubernatorial appointment (Massachusetts, New Hampshire, and Rhode Island), justices hold office for life or until a mandatory retirement age.

Retention elections are nonetheless elections, and organized opposition to sitting justices has become more common in states with this feature. Retention elections have changed in ways similar to regular judicial elections, with a larger (though still small) number of issue-based challenges to incumbent supreme court justices. The prototype was the successful 1986 campaign to defeat three California Supreme Court justices on the ground that they consistently voted to overturn death sentences (Wold and Culver 1987). But because retention elections are usually part of the Missouri Plan system, most commentators have focused on partisan and nonpartisan elections in their assessments of elections as a means to choose judges. In discussing judicial elections, we will generally leave retention elections aside.

There was (and is) a widespread perception that campaigns for judgeships and the process of electing judges were not particularly interesting or exciting prior to the current era. In fact, one journalist compared judicial elections to playing a game of checkers through the mail (Bayne 2000). The accuracy of this perception varied by era, by state, and by level of judgeship. At the supreme court level, judicial elections were more competitive and sometimes more heated than many observers realized (Dubois 1980; Kritzer 2015). Still, the scale and vigor of campaigns were typically more limited than was true of campaigns for governor and legislative seats.

Perhaps most noteworthy was the limited activity of political interest groups, which often remained on the sidelines, even though court decisions had considerable impact on the interests of significant groups. It may be that group leaders were slow to recognize that impact. Whatever the reason, they preferred to devote most of their attention to presidential, congressional, gubernatorial, or state legislative elections.

As a result, judicial candidates typically raised little money and thus found it difficult to get their message to the public, a situation that reinforced the impression that judicial elections were unimportant. Moreover, many judicial candidates resisted campaigning as being beneath a judge's dignity. Those judicial candidates who embraced campaigning were often bound by state statutes and rules of conduct that limited what they could say on the campaign trail, restricted their ability to engage in partisan events, or prevented them from raising money directly from donors. Legal organizations such as the American Bar Association and American Judicature Society preferred these legal and practical limitations on campaigns because of their concerns about the potential consequences of more active and issue-oriented judicial campaigns, including their impact on the legitimacy of the courts in the eyes of the public.

Slowly, the relatively quiet nature of judicial elections began to change.

Organized interests began to realize that it was much more efficient to try to influence a group of five, seven, or nine justices than it was to persuade a much larger Congress or state legislature to support their causes. Furthermore, on many issues, such as medical malpractice or immunity from lawsuits for certain individuals and institutions, judges actually had greater impact on state policy than legislators. As a result, interest groups began to focus on these races. Especially important were business groups that responded to the electoral success of labor-supported supreme court candidates and to unfavorable doctrinal trends in supreme courts (Shugerman 2012, 241).

Events in the state of Ohio during the late 1970s and early 1980s illustrate this process very well. Historically, the Ohio Supreme Court had been a relatively conservative body that was generally supportive of business interests. In 1978, the partisan makeup of the court flipped, and the Democrats obtained a 4-3 majority, which eventually grew to 6-1. The new court was led by the controversial chief justice Frank Celebrezze, whose brother James joined the court in 1982. Tarr and Porter (1988, 128–29) note the sudden shift in decisions once the Democrats achieved a majority. As they describe it, the court began reversing a "long line of precedent" that had imposed "restrictions on suits against state and local governments and limitations on medical malpractice claims and the rights of tenants, consumers, and workers injured during the course of employment. . . . Virtually overnight the court became 'pro-labor and highly urban' in orientation" (see also Lopeman 1999, 71–74).

As a result of the court's policy shift, business groups, including the Ohio Chamber of Commerce and the Ohio Manufacturers' Association, attempted to remove the Celebrezze brothers from the bench and return the court to a Republican majority.[8] The result was a set of high-profile contests for seats on the court in 1984 and 1986 that featured unusually high levels of interest group involvement, spending, and news coverage (Tarr and Porter 1988, 171–76; Baum 1987, 1988–89). These groups helped bring about the defeat of James Celebrezze and another Democratic judicial candidate, John E. Corrigan, in 1984. In 1986, Republican Thomas Moyer defeated Frank Celebrezze, and the Ohio Supreme Court gained a Republican majority that has continued since that time.

Ohio was not the only state where interest groups were increasingly active in judicial elections. Yet most judicial elections still remained out of the spotlight, largely because of the lack of interest group involvement. Between 1990 and 2000, even with substantial increases in spending in some states, the median amount of money raised by supreme court candidates was only about $150,000 in partisan contests and $50,000 in nonpartisan contests (Goldberg, Holman, and Sanchez 2002, 12). And it remained true that a substantial proportion of incumbents faced no opponents or won by large margins, especially in states with nonpartisan elections (Kritzer 2015, 117).

It was around this time, however, that scholars associated with Justice at Stake, an umbrella organization concerned about changes in judicial campaigns, issued the first of what would become biennial reports on the previous cycle of supreme court elections. This report, titled *The New Politics of Judicial Elections: How 2000 Was a Watershed Year for Big Money, Special Interest Pressure, and TV Advertising in State Supreme Court Campaigns,* documented a 61 percent increase in judicial candidate fundraising between 1998 and 2000 and more than $10 million spent on advertising in 2000 (Goldberg, Holman, and Sanchez 2002, 5). "Americans want their judges to be fair and impartial, period," write the authors of the report. "But the new politics of judicial campaigns . . . heightens one of the public's greatest fears: that the judges who protect their individual rights will be making decisions with one eye on a growing tide of campaign donors, special interests, and attack ads. In a number of key battleground states, 2000 was clearly a wake-up call. Unless citizens and their leaders come together, the threat to fair and impartial justice will grow, perhaps rapidly" (Goldberg, Holman, and Sanchez 2002, 6).[9]

The perception of a substantial change in the character of supreme court elections has triggered a normative debate about the desirability of this change and, more fundamentally, about the desirability of judicial elections themselves. For legal scholars and others who were already skeptical of the practice of electing judges, the development of new-style campaigns for judgeships has made a bad situation even worse (Geyh 2003). But some defenders of judicial elections have argued that new-style supreme court elections are not problematic and may even have positive effects (Bonneau and Hall 2009; Gibson 2012).

This debate is symbolized by the US Supreme Court's 2002 decision in *Republican Party v. White* declaring that Minnesota's "announce clause," which limited the discussion of policy issues by judicial candidates, violated the First Amendment. The Court divided 5-4, and the majority opinion by Justice Antonin Scalia differed sharply in its assessment of issue-oriented judicial campaigns from the dissents by Justices Ruth Bader Ginsburg and John Paul Stevens. Scalia quoted a prior decision by the Court: "It is simply not the function of the government to select which issues are worth discussing or debating in the course of a political campaign." He added that "we have never allowed the government to prohibit candidates from communicating relevant information to voters during an election."[10] Still another point of view was expressed by Justice Sandra Day O'Connor, who concurred with the Court's decision but wrote separately "to express my concerns about judicial elections generally."[11]

We should not assume that observers of judicial elections are correct in their perception of change in the character of those elections, because that perception is based in part on some well-publicized episodes. In the past decade, for instance, a series of contentious supreme court campaigns in Michigan and Wisconsin has attracted considerable attention (Baum 2012, 109–10; Kritzer 2015, 17–21). In the most widely noted episode in the country, the head of a coal company with a high-stakes case pending before the West Virginia Supreme Court spent an estimated $3.5 million in a successful 2004 campaign to defeat incumbent justice Warren McGraw, using a massive television ad campaign to portray the incumbent as soft on crime (Stern 2005). The Karmeier-Maag contest referred to at the beginning of this chapter was another high-profile race that drew the ire of opponents of judicial elections. Such vivid examples can be misleading.

Yet, as the biennial *New Politics* reports document, the perceptions of change in the character of supreme court campaigns and the involvement of interest groups in those campaigns clearly have considerable validity.[12] Data on spending by candidates show that campaigns, on average, have indeed become costlier and that growth in spending has been augmented by spending on behalf of candidates by political parties and interest groups. In 1989–90, according to one analysis, supreme court candidates raised about $6 million for their campaigns; in 1991–92, they raised about $9.5 million. In contrast, in every biennium from 1997–98 to 2011–12 the total was more than $27 million, and in three of those eight bienniums the total was more than $45 million (Sample et al. 2010, 5; Skaggs et al. 2011, 5; Bannon, Velasco, and Casey 2013, 6). One study of the ten states with the highest levels of spending in 2009–10 estimated that about 30 percent of all spending was by parties and interest groups independent of the candidates (Skaggs et al. 2011, 5).[13]

The evidence on whether campaigns have become "nastier" and "noisier" is less systematic, but in these respects as well there are clear indications of change. In itself, the growth in spending has enabled candidates and their supporters to make campaigns more visible to the voters. Although data on the tone of television commercials go back only to

2000, attack ads come disproportionately from interest groups that operate independently of candidates' campaigns (Goldberg, Holman, and Sanchez 2002, 17; Skaggs et al. 2011, 16; M. G. Hall 2015, 85), and such independent efforts are a relatively recent phenomenon. Similarly, since 2000 a substantial proportion of commercials emphasize issues of judicial policy, with candidates and their supporters touting their own policy positions or ascribing unpopular positions to their opponents (Goldberg, Holman, and Sanchez 2002, 25–26; Sample et al. 2010, 86–97). This, too, appears to be a departure from an earlier pattern of ads that emphasized candidates' personal qualities.

In light of the strong theme of change in the character of supreme court contests, it is important to stress that these changes have been uneven, especially as they relate to interest group involvement. Campaigns for supreme court seats have changed in some states more than others and fluctuate in their scale and content from one election year to another within a state and even in the same state and election year. Moreover, there has been greater continuity in the attributes of supreme court elections over time than many observers acknowledge (M. G. Hall 2015, chap. 2). Still, in the aggregate, the changes in supreme court campaigns have been considerable. The process of running for positions on state supreme courts is quite different today from what it was a few decades ago. Any contemporary study of judicial elections must give careful attention to these changes.

Shifting the Focus to Judicial Policy

There was significant scholarship in the past on the election of judges as well as a body of writing that evaluated the functioning of judicial elections and offered proposals for changes in selection systems. However, the growing visibility of supreme court contests has spurred an unprecedented volume of academic research on judicial elections and debate about normative issues that arise from changes in judicial elections.

This body of work is informative and valuable. It documents changes in the scope and character of campaigns for seats on state supreme courts (e.g., M. G. Hall 2015), it probes patterns in voting behavior in supreme court contests (e.g., Bonneau and Cann 2015; Kritzer 2015), and it tells us something about how new-style elections affect public attitudes toward the courts (e.g., Gibson 2012). We will make extensive use of this scholarship in the chapters to follow.

While doing so, we focus our attention on the broader context of judicial elections. Our concern is linkages among campaigns, the voters, and the policies that are made by state supreme courts. The connection between campaigns and voters is important, and we seek to illuminate how voters respond to the efforts of interest groups to influence their choices. As suggested earlier, we are even more interested in the linkages that involve the policies made by supreme courts: how those policies stimulate campaign activity and how voters' collective decisions influence supreme court policy.

That last linkage is of particular interest to us because what ultimately is at stake in the election of judges is judicial policy. The opinions of state supreme courts contain statements of law that often determine the rights and obligations of thousands or even millions of individuals and organizations. Returning to the Karmeier-Maag contest at the beginning of this introduction, the effort by State Farm to secure a favorable outcome of its own case was important, but considerably more consequential was the perceived impact of the Illinois Supreme Court's prospective decision on a large number of disputes between companies and consumers, many of them involving substantial sums of money. It was this broader impact that attracted the attention of a range of interest groups and led many of them to participate in the case through the submission of amicus briefs.

The decisions made by state supreme courts range across a wide array of policy areas, including criminal justice, the family, civil liberties, contracts, and torts. In each of these areas, even single decisions of state courts can establish legal rules that have fundamental effects on the lives of many people. Thus, what matters the most about judicial elections is how they affect the legal rules that supreme courts make.

The existing scholarship has given considerable attention to one way in which elections can affect policy: through the impact of electoral considerations on sitting justices' votes.[14] One body of research analyzes the relationship between campaign contributions and justices' votes in cases in which contributors have an interest and seeks to determine whether there is a causal relationship between contributions and votes (see, e.g., Cann 2007; McCall and McCall 2007; Kang and Shepherd 2011).[15] Another body of research, primarily on criminal cases, analyzes how public attitudes and perceived threats to reelection affect justices' votes (see, e.g., Brace and Boyea 2008; Caldarone, Canes-Wrone, and Clark 2009; Canes-Wrone, Clark, and Kelly 2014).

As important as this body of research is, it reaches only one of the links between elections and judicial policy. The votes in supreme court cases are influenced significantly by which people sit on a court even when external pressures on those justices are strong (Langer 2002, chap.

5; Brace and Boyea 2008, 369; Caldarone, Canes-Wrone, and Clark 2009, 568). In turn, the most consequential function of supreme court elections is the determination of which people will serve on their states' highest courts. That function is demonstrated by the very substantial difference it can make whether one candidate or the other wins supreme court election contests (Baum, Gray, and Klein 2017).

Of course, individual votes are not in the end what matter most to interest groups—or to lawyers, litigants, and the general public. What matter most are case outcomes and, even more, a court's opinions. It is through opinions and patterns of outcomes that courts shape the legal landscape. But even a single justice often has considerable impact on a supreme court's collective decisions.

This brings us back to the question of linkages. If legal policy is the most important thing about judicial elections, and if the content of legal policy is largely determined by the membership of state supreme courts, then the linkages among campaigns, voting, court membership, and court policy should be at the center of discussions of judicial elections.

Let us start with campaigning and specifically with the origins of the new-style judicial campaigns. Certainly recent changes in law and politics, such as the *White* ruling, may have had an impact on supreme court campaigns. But they cannot provide anything like a complete explanation of the origins of new-style campaigns. It is important to keep in mind that Schotland's observation about noisier, nastier, and costlier judicial campaigns came in 1985. And interest groups have always had the ability to speak in favor of various candidates and policies or against them. An understanding of the change in the character of judicial campaigns requires us to go back considerably farther than the last decade.

In our view, the rise of new-style supreme court campaigns has multiple sources. But as we have already suggested, the primary source was a growing perception of the importance of state supreme courts to the goals of major economic interest groups. The monetary contributions and independent expenditures that enabled large-scale campaigns and that facilitated a change in the content of those campaigns were driven by a desire to influence supreme court policy by shaping the membership of courts. Focusing on the policies supreme courts make helps us understand not only the changes in campaigns over time, but also variation in the scope and character of campaigns across and even within states. That variation can be understood as a product of strategic considerations by interest groups, which invest resources in supreme court contests when they see the best opportunity to affect policies that concern them.

Voters play a key role in linking campaign activity to changes in court policy. When groups seek to obtain more favorable court policy by electing or reelecting supportive justices, they are trying to influence the decisions of individual voters whether to participate in a particular supreme court contest and their choices between competing candidates. Of course, success in those efforts is not guaranteed, especially when groups on one side of an issue face opposition from groups on the other side.

Voters' roles in the process are of particular interest in light of the general view that voters in judicial contests are not well informed (see, e.g., Johnson, Schaefer, and McKnight 1978; Lovrich and Sheldon 1983; but see Bonneau and Hall 2009). If this is the case, how can interest groups and others involved in campaigns communicate to voters information about judicial policy on which they might act? We need a better understanding of the kinds of information that organized interests are conveying to voters and whether voters are using that information when deciding whether to participate and how to vote. In other words, how are organized interests successful—or not successful—in convincing voters to elect candidates who will shape the direction of the court in a way that is consistent with the wishes of those groups?

Even if groups are successful in their efforts to shape the membership of supreme courts through elections, it is not guaranteed that they will get the policies they want. Just as presidents can make mistakes in choosing Supreme Court justices, groups can make mistakes in backing judicial candidates. Moreover, factors other than the policy views of individual justices can shape supreme court policies. It seems reasonable to assume that election outcomes influence supreme court policy, but well-informed debates about judicial elections and other methods of selection require rigorous testing of this assumption.

To summarize, we are interested in three broad questions concerning the relationship between elections and judicial policy:

1. How do the policies of state supreme courts affect election campaigns for seats on those courts?
2. How does campaign activity shape supreme court policy through election outcomes?
3. What role do voters play in linking campaign activity to supreme court policy?

When answering these questions, one can think about a cycle that links policy, election outcomes, campaigns, and voters together. Policy change on a specific issue occurs on the court, which in turn can spark interest group activity from the losing side to try to change the makeup of the court via campaigns. Interest groups provide campaign contributions to parties and candidates who support their causes, spend independently on behalf of candidates who support their causes (or conversely against those in opposition), and mobilize supporters on behalf of their preferred candidates. If these efforts are successful, voters will elect candidates who support the group's interest. Whether voters who do so act consciously on behalf of the group's interest is another matter—and one that merits attention. Election outcomes then shape the makeup of the court, which influences policy, and the cycle can begin all over again.

Why Ohio and Torts?

To answer our three broad questions and to understand the linkages among judicial campaigns, election outcomes, and public policy, we turn to tort law in the state of Ohio. What a single-state study lacks in breadth, it gains in depth. There is considerable value to multistate studies of specific phenomena, such as the scope and content of supreme court campaigns or the behavior of voters in elections of supreme court justices. But to gain a full sense of the series of linkages that we have described, we need to look closely at what happened in one state over a substantial period of time. Such a study can be accomplished even in a single state only under unusual conditions, and analogous multistate studies would be exceedingly difficult to carry out.

Ohio is an attractive state to study for two reasons. First, Ohio experienced a long-term effort to reshape supreme court policies through elections. Responding to a sharp leftward turn in the Ohio Supreme Court's policies on personal injury law and other economic issues, business groups and their allies began an effort to move the court in a conservative direction in the early eighties. Initial successes in 1984 and 1986 were followed by a slower process of consolidating the gains achieved in those two election years. This effort, and the reaction to it by groups on the other side of the ideological and partisan divide, transformed supreme court elections in Ohio. But even during this fierce campaign for control of the Ohio Supreme Court, some battles were far more intense than others.

Second, Ohio provides a unique opportunity to probe the role of voters in linking campaign efforts to policy change. We are able to take advantage of a series of election surveys conducted in eight election years between 1984 and 2006, a series that has no equivalent in other states. In broad terms, these data allow us to test how the involvement of interest groups in supreme court contests affects voters' participation in those contests and their choices between candidates. Further, they enable us to probe voters' role in the linkage between elections and policy: to what extent did voters act deliberately to bring about changes in the tort policies of the Ohio Supreme Court?

In analyzing judicial elections in Ohio, we take into account developments and research findings about other states. By doing so, we can put the Ohio experience in a broader perspective. But to take advantage of the depth that a single-state study allows, we give the preponderance of our attention to Ohio.

We have also chosen to analyze torts. Certainly there are numerous issues on which one could focus. Indeed, issues other than torts, including crime and gay rights, have been at the center of some judicial election contests. Yet the new-style campaigns have been driven more than anything else by battles over torts. Indeed, business and trial lawyers are regularly the two groups donating the largest amounts to judicial candidates (Sample et al. 2010). Both have a great deal at stake in cases involving economic issues, and their stakes in personal injury law are especially high. Ohio exemplifies the primary place of torts in issue-driven campaigns for state supreme courts.

Our focus on a single issue area in one state allows us to analyze court policies in unusual depth. We created a dataset of information on all tort decisions relevant to the business community over four decades, from 1973 through 2012. That dataset allows us to analyze patterns in court policies and the voting behavior of individual justices over time in a way that has not been possible in the past. We use the dataset to trace the developments that spurred new-style supreme court campaigns in Ohio and to engage in a systematic investigation of the effects of supreme court elections on judicial policy.

Some general information about the Ohio Supreme Court will be useful as background. Because Ohio has an intermediate court of appeals, the jurisdiction of its supreme court over most types of cases is discretionary. However, the court has mandatory jurisdiction over some types of cases, including appeals from death sentences and from the decisions of some administrative agencies. The court is also final arbiter of discipline of attorneys, and discipline cases constitute a significant portion of its work.

The supreme court has seven justices, the most common size of state supreme courts. The chief justice and six associate justices are all elected for six-year terms. The terms are staggered so that two associate justices are chosen in November of each even-numbered year. The governor unilaterally fills any vacancy that arises during a justice's term, with the appointee running in the next general election in an even-numbered year for the remainder of the term. To be eligible for election, a candidate must have practiced law for at least six years and must not be more than seventy years old when the new term would begin. As will become clear in the chapters that follow, the mandatory retirement rule played an important role during our study period, with several justices forced to leave the bench because of it.

Ohio's formal system for electing judges is unusual in that it combines a partisan primary election with a nonpartisan general election. Only Arizona (which no longer elects appellate judges) uses the same system, although Michigan combines a partisan nominating procedure—party conventions—with a nonpartisan general election.[16] What would seem to be an anomalous combination of procedures at the two stages of election resulted from two Progressive era reforms in 1910 and 1912 that replaced partisan with nonpartisan general elections and nomination by party conventions with partisan primary elections (Aumann 1931, 412–14).[17] The system created by those reforms has survived a long series of efforts to modify or eliminate it, including two public votes on adoption of the Missouri Plan and a recent federal lawsuit to require that candidates' party affiliations be listed on the general election ballot.[18]

Although the absence of party labels on the general election ballot has considerable effect on voters, in practice Ohio's supreme court elections have much in common with those in many of the states that use partisan elections to choose supreme court justices. Even in states with fully nonpartisan systems, competing candidates in those states are often Republicans and Democrats (Dubois 1980, chap. 3; Kritzer 2015, chap. 6), and party organizations participate in campaigns a good deal.[19] The partisan primary in Ohio encourages involvement by party organizations, and it also exposes primary election voters to the name of their party's nominee.[20]

In the chapters that follow, we necessarily discuss the course of campaigns, elections, and tort policy in Ohio with some specificity. In following that course, readers may find it useful to refer to the appendices at the end of the book. Appendix 1 provides information about the justices who served on the Ohio Supreme Court from 1981 to the present and the interest groups that participated in supreme court elections during that period. Appendix 2 summarizes the candidates and outcomes of supreme court elections from 1976 through 2014. Appendix 3 shows the membership of the court from 1977 through 2017 in terms of party affiliation and, for the Republican justices, in terms of their positions on tort policy. The balance on the court between pro-plaintiff and pro-defendant justices is at the heart of our concern, because the balance at any given time spurred electoral activity and determined the general tenor of the court's policies.

Overview of the Book

The rest of the book consists of three substantive chapters and a conclusion that addresses the normative implications of our findings.

Chapter 1 is about the content of Ohio Supreme Court tort policy. Focusing primarily on the years 1973–2012, we first examine case outcomes and doctrinal change, before turning to the decision making of individual justices. At the level of the court, we dissect trends in plaintiff and defense win rates in all cases involving tort issues. We do the same in examining the court's decisions in overruling precedent.

By laying out patterns in the court's tort policies, we provide a picture of the status quo to which interest groups responded at a given time. But our central concern is the impact that election outcomes have on public policy. We take advantage of new analytic methods to perform tests to determine the consequences for tort policy of having one justice sit on the court as opposed to another. By doing so, we assess the extent to which groups that participate in electoral contests for the supreme court get what they want from the court when their favored candidates win.

Based on the changes to tort policy analyzed in chapter 1, we examine the responses of interest group activity to those decisions in chapter 2. Focusing on the period since 1977, we give particular attention to variation in the conduct of campaigns, especially as it relates to interest groups. We develop a set of expectations regarding the conditions in which we would expect high levels of interest group activity in judicial elections and then trace that activity over several eras related to the Ohio Supreme Court.

In chapter 3, we document the role that voters play in linking elections and policy, analyzing elections between 1980 and 2014. We begin by examining the impact of group-driven campaign activity on candidates' shares of the vote. Finding that interest groups' efforts affect election outcomes, we probe the sources of that effect by analyzing voters' decisions whether to participate in supreme court contests (i.e., "roll-off") and their choices between competing candidates.

As we have indicated, we are especially interested in voters' intent.

If rulings on torts have changed as a result of interest group activity in elections, have voters been knowing participants in this change? We use information from our surveys of voters to address that question.

Finally, in chapter 4 we focus on the implications of our findings. We consider what the findings tell us about the relationship between judicial policy and judicial elections and about the role of the voters in linking the two. We also consider how the findings contribute to the normative debate over the wisdom of electing judges, using our study to provide a new perspective on that debate.

ONE

The Course of Tort Policy

At one time, especially before World War II, the Ohio Supreme Court was quicker than the average state supreme court to adopt new tort law doctrines that favored plaintiffs (Canon and Baum 1981). By the 1970s, however, tort law in Ohio was in a rather sleepy state. The Ohio court still made major changes in the law on occasion. In 1975, for instance, it invalidated the state guest statute, which exempted a driver from liability toward a guest in the car if the guest was not paying for the ride.[1] But more typical of this period were decisions that refused to adopt proposed changes in the law. The court chose not to overrule spousal immunity, the prohibition of lawsuits between spouses (1978); not to expand the definition of "pecuniary injury" in a wrongful death statute to include loss of companionship (1979); and not to read the Landlords and Tenants Act of 1974 as establishing "duties or standards of conduct for the breach of which a tenant may hold his landlord liable in tort" (1980).[2]

Those three decisions were consistent with the court's tendency to favor defendants over plaintiffs in tort law, but that tendency was not overwhelming. Each of the three decisions attracted dissents from justices who favored changes in the law, but on the whole disagreements on the court were low key. In this sense, too, the court's work in personal injury law was quiet.

All of this changed beginning in the early 1980s. Pro-plaintiff justices engaged in a decades-long battle with the state legislature and succeeded in swinging the court to the left—first in the early 1980s and then, after a reversal of direction, a second time in the 1990s. The justices became more polarized, sometimes engaging in sharp verbal battles through their opinions. "Stare decisis" became little more than a phrase of lament. Things eventually quieted back down, but only after the court had turned sharply, and lastingly, back to the right.

In this chapter we canvass these changes and attempt to determine to what extent they are attributable to changes in the court's membership. We begin with a qualitative overview of doctrine and opinion language before moving to quantitative analyses of justices' votes.

Changing Doctrine

The topic of immunity from liability provides an excellent example of changing doctrine. As of 1972, immunity was commonly available as a defense to tort claims in Ohio. Even when they were plainly at fault, governments and charities could often get lawsuits dismissed simply by virtue of their status. Insurance companies could invoke interspousal and parent-child immunity to avoid payouts when the victim was injured by a relative (usually in a car accident). The landscape of immunity changed dramatically with a series of decisions in the mid-1980s. Major legislation and court decisions since then have been more favorable to defendants, but immunity has not returned to pre-1972 levels.

Both charitable and intrafamilial immunity had been created through court decisions many years before the period under study and were based on both moral and public policy judgments. Then, as now, charities and families were valued for providing support to people when they most need and can least afford it, and it was thought that both types of institutions could be undermined by allowing beneficiaries of support to sue benefactors. In addition, lawsuits within families raised concerns about collusive fraud.

By the 1970s, the spread of liability insurance had done much to allay these fears (though not the fear of fraud). Lawsuits were still directed against charities and family members in name, but in reality it was insurance companies who were on the hook. Charitable immunity, especially, was on shaky ground, having been limited by a series of decisions in the previous several decades. Perhaps most importantly, in 1956 the court had abolished charitable immunity for hospitals.[3] So the court's decision to abolish charitable immunity altogether in 1984, with only Justices Robert Holmes and Ralph Locher dissenting, probably did not come as much of a surprise.[4]

In contrast, intrafamilial immunity retained considerable vitality until just before it was abolished. The court explicitly reaffirmed both spousal and parent-child immunity as late as 1982, in the latter case refusing to make an exception even where "the parent alleged to be negligent is deceased and liability insurance proceeds alone would be the source for the payment of any judgment."[5]

Within two years, however, familial immunity was clearly under threat. In 1983, the court ruled that spousal immunity did not bar an action for wrongful death brought by the estate of the deceased spouse against the surviving spouse.[6] (The practical effect in that case was to allow the husband, who caused the accident, to recover from his insurance company by suing himself.) The next year, it overruled the 1982 case on parental liability and held that an unemancipated child could sue a dead parent's estate.[7]

The court did not allow the suspense to build for long, fully abolishing the immunity of both parents and children in 1984 and spousal immunity in July, 1985.[8] James Celebrezze, newly arrived on the court, joined with William Brown, Clifford Brown, and A. William Sweeney to form a bare majority for abolition. Strikingly, James Celebrezze was not accompanied by his brother Frank, who, while vociferously pro-plaintiff by this point in his career, was something of a social conservative. In fact, Frank wrote the principal dissent in the case abolishing parent-child immunity. (However, he accepted the rulings as a matter of stare decisis in later cases.)

Whereas the court had the stage largely to itself when it came to charitable and family immunity, the legislature had a starring role in the story of governmental immunity. By the start of the period covered by our study, it was well established that governmental immunity was only available when the defendant had been engaged in a "governmental"—as opposed to a "proprietary"—function. Indeed, the court issued an important decision limiting municipal immunity in 1972, holding that "where a municipality owns a hospital, thereby providing a service not essential to municipal government, there is no basis in logic for granting the municipality governmental immunity as to that hospital."[9]

Nevertheless, governmental immunity was still an important barrier to lawsuits. The very next year the court, in a 4-3 decision, relied on statements in precedent to rule that state—as opposed to municipal—immunity is absolute except where the state consents to be sued through legislation and that the Ohio State University hospitals were immune to suit.[10]

The first and biggest blow against governmental immunity came from the legislature, when it passed an act in 1974 waiving sovereign immunity for all institutions and instrumentalities of the state government. The act specifically exempted political subdivisions, such as municipalities and school districts, from this waiver, leaving them with the immunity already recognized in case law. However, the court restricted subdivisions' immunity dramatically in a series of cases decided between 1981 and 1984. Having first declared that it possessed the "constitutional authority to modify or abrogate common law doctrines of governmental or sovereign immunity," it went on to abolish common-law immunity for boards of education, park districts, and public libraries, and for municipalities with the exception of "essential acts of governmental decision-making."[11] These cases were decided by consistent 5-2 voting blocs, with the Celebrezze brothers, the Browns, and Sweeney in the majority and Justices Holmes and Locher in dissent.

In a pattern that would play out in numerous other areas of tort law, the tide then turned once more, as the legislature responded to the court's pro-plaintiff decisions with legislation to protect defendants. It began by granting political subdivisions substantial statutory immunity in 1985; later amendments expanded that immunity considerably. These laws and the decisions implementing them elicited fierce protests from some justices, especially Paul Pfeifer. ("With its decision today, the court has stated: 'The Constitution be damned, we will not allow the King or any person exercising discretion on behalf of the King to be sued.' Even though Ohio's citizens have been part of a representative democracy for over 200 years, the King still lives."[12]) However, the critics on the court never formed a majority, and the law in Ohio today is that a political subdivision can be sued only for certain discretionary acts, and only if those discretionary acts were performed "with malicious purpose, in bad faith, or in a wanton or reckless manner."[13]

INTENTIONAL TORTS BY EMPLOYERS

Ohio's system of workers' compensation (originally "workmen's" compensation) was established in the early 1910s through statutes and a constitutional amendment.[14] Like all such systems, it requires employers to pay into insurance funds that are used to compensate workers injured on the job. Its generally understood purposes were not only to provide more financial security to workers, but also to make compensation more predictable for both employees and employers and to relieve the courts of a large number of cases. Accordingly, the Ohio Code as of the 1970s exempted employers who complied with the law from having to "respond in damages at common law or by statute for any injury, or occupational disease, or bodily condition, received or contracted by any employee in the course of or arising out of his employment."[15]

In 1982, the court was asked to declare that this exempting language was not absolute—specifically, that an injured worker could sue an employer for damages for an intentional tort. Justices Robert Holmes and Blanche Krupansky, emphasizing the goals of predictability and reducing judicial caseloads, would have held that intentional torts, like ordinary acts of negligence, must be handled exclusively through the workers' compensation system. But five justices disagreed and ruled that suits for intentional torts could be brought in court.[16]

Two years later the court went further, in a decision that fractured the coalition from the previous case. The court announced two major holdings. First, a successful suit did not require a finding of a specific intent to injure; an act "committed with the belief that [an] injury is substantially certain to occur" would also constitute an intentional tort. Second, the fact that the employee had already received workers' compensation benefits for the injury did not preclude a lawsuit nor reduce the amount of damages for which the employer could be held liable.[17] Justices Ralph Locher and William Brown had been in the majority that allowed suits for intentional torts by employers. Here, while Locher agreed with the first holding and Brown did not indicate a view one way or the other, both joined with Justice Holmes in dissenting from the second holding. The fourth vote for the majority came from James Celebrezze, who had replaced Krupansky.

Employees did not win every case in the next two decades. For instance, a unanimous court in 1988 warned litigants that claims against employers would be dismissed unless "the complaint alleges facts showing that the employer: (1) specifically desired to injure the employee; or (2) knew that injury to an employee was certain or substantially certain to result from the employer's act and despite this knowledge, still proceeded."[18] However, most major decisions went in favor of workers.

Most importantly, when the state legislature tried to restrict suits against employers, the court refused to allow it. A 1986 statute set limits on the damages that could be awarded for an intentional tort and gave the workers' compensation commission—as opposed to the courts—exclusive authority to determine damages. The court struck the statute down in its entirety in 1991, ruling 4-3 that the statute went beyond the power allocated to the legislature in the Ohio constitution.[19] The legislature responded in 1995 with a less direct assault on the court's position, recognizing a claim of intentional tort while attempting to set fairly strict parameters on the claim. Notably, the statute required plaintiffs to demonstrate the elements of an intentional tort by "clear and convincing evidence," a more demanding standard than the typical "preponderance of the evidence." Again the court invalidated the entire statute by a 4-3 vote.[20]

Neither the legislature nor the pro-plaintiff majority on the court tried to disguise the fact that they were in a struggle to control tort policy. The 1995 statute explicitly declared the legislature's "intent . . . to supersede" several court decisions. Justice Andrew Douglas's majority opinion striking down that statute in 1999 upbraided the legislature: "In [invalidating the 1991 statute,] we thought that we had made it abundantly clear that any statute created to provide employers with immunity from liability for their intentional tortious conduct cannot withstand constitutional scrutiny. Notwithstanding, the General Assembly has enacted *R.C. 2745.01,* and, again, seeks to cloak employers with immunity. In this regard, we can only assume that the General Assembly has either failed to grasp the import of our holdings in *Brady* or that the General Assembly has simply elected to willfully disregard that decision."[21]

The legislature's next attempt to limit the scope of intentional tort suits against employers came in a 2005 statute. In a creative move, the legislature recognized a cause of action if an employer "committed [a] tortious act with the intent to injure another or with the belief that the injury was substantially certain to occur" but then defined away the second alternative by declaring "substantially certain" to mean "that an employer acts with deliberate intent to cause an employee to suffer an injury, a disease, a condition, or death." Two Ohio courts of appeals balked at the legislature's sleight of hand, one ruling that the statute was unconstitutional, the other that the definition of "substantially certain" was a drafting error. But the membership of the supreme court had changed a great deal by 2010, and the legislature won both cases when they reached that court, with only Justice Pfeifer dissenting and with several cases explicitly or implicitly overruled in the process.[22]

THE COURT VERSUS THE LEGISLATURE

Public battles with the legislature were a regular feature of court life from the 1980s through the early 2000s. The single most consequential, and perhaps the fiercest, battle took place outside the area of torts (Hignett 2005; Obhof 2005). In 1997 the court held that Ohio's system for funding elementary and secondary schools created inequities that violated the Ohio Constitution's requirement of a "thorough and efficient" public education system. That decision spurred a half dozen years of conflict between the court and the legislature, in which the legislature made some changes to the funding system and the court twice found the changes inadequate. Ultimately a more conservative court retreated in 2003, holding that the funding system was still unconstitutional but denying any further enforcement of that holding.[23]

However, torts and insurance policy dominated the struggle. In addition to those issues we have already described, the court and legislature fought over when auto policyholders were entitled to receive compensation under uninsured motorist provisions and how much they could receive, the adequacy of statutes of limitations and repose (especially in medical malpractice), and limits on damages, whether through direct caps or through "collateral source" rules that required plaintiffs' awards to be reduced when they received compensation from other sources.[24]

The most dramatic confrontation came after the legislature's passage, in 1996, of a vast statute encompassing all of these areas plus many more. (According to the court, the new statute "amend[ed], enact[ed], or repeal[ed] over one hundred sections of the Ohio Revised Code."[25]) Not only did the statute attempt to undo a number of constitutional rulings of the court, the legislature expressly stated its intent to do so, naming specific cases and indicating a preference for the reasoning in dissents and lower court opinions.

In 1999, Justice Alice Robie Resnick, joined by three other justices, wrote the opinion of the court striking down the entire act as a violation of separation of powers.[26] Although to this point in her career Resnick had shown far less of an inclination to heated rhetoric than, say, Andrew Douglas, Clifford Brown, or Paul Pfeifer, the anger in this opinion is nearly palpable from its first line, a heading entitled "Am.Sub.H.B. No. 350 Converts the Drive for Civil Justice Reform into an Attack on the Judiciary as a Coordinate Branch of Government." Just as notable was the court's willingness to decide the case. The case did not arise out of a claim for damages; rather, it was a mandamus action brought by the Ohio Academy of Trial Lawyers and the Ohio AFL-CIO requesting that the supreme court prohibit lower court judges from applying the provisions of the statute in their courtrooms. The majority's willingness to decide the case in this posture despite the serious questions raised about standing and ripeness was as strong an indication of its view of the legislature's actions as the language used in the opinion.

As forceful as the court's action was, it could not stand against continued legislative pressure and changes in the court's composition. Over the next several years, the legislature, while using less confrontational language, essentially reenacted several of the provisions that had been struck by the court. In 2007 the court upheld limits on punitive damages and noneconomic compensatory damages (for pain and suffering, e.g.) over objections that they violated the right to a jury trial in the Ohio Constitution.[27] In 2008 and 2012, it upheld statutes of repose that barred most product liability claims brought more than ten years after acquisition of the product and most medical malpractice claims filed more than four years after the alleged malpractice occurred.[28]

The last of these decisions elicited this protest from Justice Pfeifer: "The sweeping language employed by the majority in this case is the crescendo in our court's decade-long deference to, and acceptance of, the General Assembly's assault on our citizens' right to remedy set forth, without alteration, for over two centuries in the Ohio Constitution" (420). Indeed, Pfeifer dissented in each of these cases. Except for one instance when he was joined by Justice Terrence O'Donnell (in voting to invalidate the cap on noneconomic compensatory damages), he dissented alone.

JUSTICE VERSUS JUSTICE

If these decisions gave the impression that the justices were divided into two camps—one allied with insurance companies, other big businesses, and the legislature, the other allied with trial lawyers and labor against the legislature—the justices did little in their opinions to dispel the impression.[29] Some actively encouraged it.

Frank Celebrezze might have been the first. The forum he chose was the annual report of sorts that he began publishing in the *Ohio Northern University Law Review* shortly after he became chief justice. These reports—which were really introductions to the journal's annual review of Ohio law—were expressly geared toward the general public, not legal practitioners, with the purpose of "inform[ing] Ohio citizens of the work of their highest court" (Celebrezze 1982, 559). The first report (in 1981) included little in the way of editorial comment, but this changed starting with the second, where the theme of the title and opening paragraphs of the report was the court's granting of new rights to Ohioans. The third report boasted that the court's opinions reflected a "progressive attitude toward the concerns of individuals as well as a willingness to depart from precedent to protect those concerns" (Celebrezze 1983, 675), and the others continued in this vein.

Prose like this can be found in the justices' official writings as well, even in opinions of the court. Here is A. William Sweeney, writing for the court in a 1981 case involving a claim for emotional distress without physical injury: "While some may view our decision today as an unsettling quantum leap into this difficult area of the law, the situation is one of paramount necessity in fitting the law to the dynamics and nuances of modern twentieth century society. We view our decision today as a bold and promising step in ensuring an individual's right to emotional tranquility."[30]

In at least one instance, a justice who supported this trend could not resist calling out colleagues who resisted it. In the 1982 decision in which the court ruled that employers could be sued for intentional torts against their employees, Frank Celebrezze wrote that he was "troubled by the language in the dissenting opinions that workers who are intentionally chemically poisoned on-the-job should not be able to recover damages from their employers because the elimination of health risks would cost too much money, thus decreasing the profits of corporations. . . . The dissenters' position is one that I would expect to be championed by a 19th century 'robber baron,' not a justice of this court who is duty-bound to serve all the people of Ohio."[31]

Naturally, some justices took a dimmer view of such steps. When, in 1981, the court overruled its narrow reading of the Landlords and Tenants Act, Justice Holmes complained: "Again we find, within this majority opinion, that the law of this state, as most recently pronounced by this court, moves rapidly through the revolving door of change, further eroding any vestige of stare decisis that might remain as a legal principle to be followed by the bench and bar of Ohio."[32] Justice Wright had this to say about a 1985 decision allowing punitive damages under uninsured motorist coverage: "In sum, I am truly disheartened by the result reached in this case since it has no foundation in law, public policy, or reason. The more one attempts to explain the result, the less one is able to understand it. The result reached today lends credence to the charge that the insurance industry has been targeted for punishment."[33]

When the pendulum swung in the other direction, it was the liberal justices who decried the abandonment of reason and precedent. This is how Justice Pfeifer responded in 2007 when the court upheld caps on punitive and noneconomic compensatory damages:

> Was there ever any doubt how this case would come out? . . . [T]oday, the members of the majority allow the evisceration of a provision of the Constitution that this court has previously stated should be jealously safeguarded . . .

> Today is a day of fulfilled expectations for insurance companies and manufacturers of defective, dangerous, or toxic products that cause injury to someone in Ohio. But this is a sad day for our Constitution and this court. And this is a tragic day for Ohioans, who no longer have any assurance that their Constitution protects the rights they cherish.[34]

Particularly striking in the quotations from Wright and Pfeifer are the explicit references to the insurance industry. Far from trying to obscure the fact that tort decision making in Ohio occurred in the context of judicial elections and interest group pressure, the justices seemed eager to call attention to it. Justice Douglas went about as far in this direction as one could imagine, concurring in another case involving uninsured motorist coverage:

> I write separately to respond, in part, to the dissent of Justice Cook. That dissent says that the majority "departs from the sound reasoning contained in *Dues* and *Tomlinson.*" I respectfully submit that the majority is doing no more than returning the law to where it was before *Dues* and *Tomlinson* were decided. The change in the law was brought about by intervening elections which placed new justices on this court. If the often-quoted (when convenient) rule of *stare decisis* had been followed, then the law in the case now before us would have remained as it was.

The opinion continues with several paragraphs expressly linking specific election results and case decisions and concludes: "Now, yet two more elections affecting this equation (November 1988 and November 1992) were held. Today, a new majority . . . returns the law to what it was before all of this started. Accordingly, I concur."[35]

Decision Making on the Court

We alluded to membership change more than once in this overview of four decades of Ohio tort law. It is hard to escape the conclusion that the huge shifts in doctrine are attributable to shifts in the court's membership. The justices seemed to separate themselves into obvious blocs in these cases, not just in their voting, but in their rhetoric: the Celebrezzes, A. William Sweeney, Clifford Brown, Francis Sweeney, Resnick, Douglas, and Pfeifer for the plaintiff; Holmes, Krupansky, Deborah Cook, Wright, Maureen O'Connor, O'Donnell, Evelyn Stratton and—to a slightly lesser extent—Moyer for the defense.

Yet it is possible to read too much into what is, importance notwithstanding, a rather small subset of all the court's decisions in this period.

To reach more confident conclusions about the effects of membership change, we need to examine the court's decisions and justices' voting more systematically. We begin at the level of the court, examining trends in plaintiff and defense win rates in all cases involving tort issues and then in the court's decisions overruling precedent. We then turn to the votes of individual justices, focusing our efforts on generating reliable inferences about the consequences of having one justice rather than another sitting on the bench.

DATA

Our dataset consists of cases decided by the Ohio Supreme Court with full opinions between 1973 and 2012. We sought to include all cases involving legal questions that carried implications for conventional tort suits pitting individuals against institutional defendants (i.e., corporations, unions, or governments), regardless of who the parties to the actual case were or whether the case itself would be considered a tort suit under the strictest definition. Thus, for instance, we included accident cases where the nominal parties were both individuals, because insurance companies' obligations—in that case and in later ones—would be affected by the decision in it. Similarly, we would include an insurance company's request for a declaratory judgment stating that it had no obligation to defend a policy holder, even though it was not technically a tort action. On the other hand, we excluded commercial torts (such as tortious interference with a contract), because they almost always involve one business against another. We also excluded libel and legal malpractice suits, as raising issues too far removed from typical cases of personal injury or property damage.[36]

Our search yielded 1,024 cases. We read each one and recorded the types of parties involved, which party won, and how each justice voted, among other things. Coding outcomes and votes was straightforward in a large majority of cases but occasionally presented challenges. The question guiding our coding was: considering all elements of the court's decision (or the individual justice's position) together, is the plaintiff or defendant in the underlying case better served by the court's decision (or by the position taken by the justice)? Where we could not answer that question confidently, we coded the result or vote as mixed.

For a first look at outcomes in the full set of cases, we show the percentage of cases won by the defendant in figure 1.1.[37] We also show the proportion of cases where at least two justices out of six or seven dissented to provide a sense of how unified or divided the court was in different

FIGURE 1.1. Patterns in outcomes of tort cases by biennium, 1973–74 through 2011–12

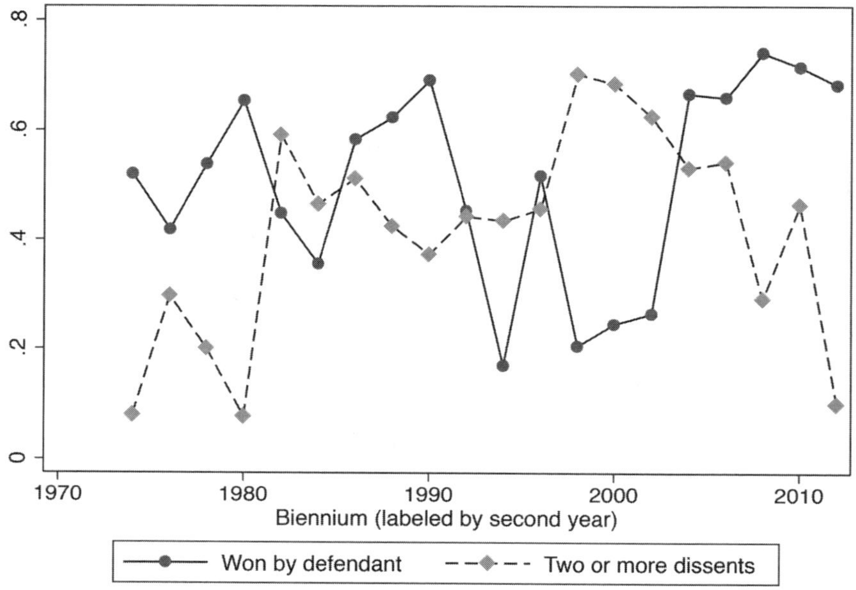

periods. Although the plots are somewhat volatile, a fairly clear picture emerges from the graph. There were two periods in which the court was highly favorable to plaintiffs—from 1981 to 1984 and in eight of the ten years between 1993 and 2002. The first move to the left brought with it a substantial increase in dissension on the court. The higher levels of dissent persisted for two decades, suggesting a long battle for control over the court's direction. The court was most deeply split at the height of the second pro-plaintiff period, around 2000. After 2002, when the court moved in a strongly pro-defendant direction, dissension fell, dramatically in the final two years, indicating that pro-defendant justices had a secure hold on the court.

To test whether this reading stands up to more rigorous scrutiny, we can regress the outcomes of individual cases on the eras we have identified from the graph. With two possible outcomes—the defendant wins or the plaintiff wins—logistic regression is the appropriate technique. The main independent variables are dummies for four of the five periods (1981–84, 1985–92, 1993–2002, 2003–12), with 1973–80 as the omitted baseline category. We control for whether the defendant was a government, whether the plaintiff was a business, whether the plaintiff was a government, and whether the defendant was the petitioner.

Holding each of the controls at its modal category, we can estimate the expected change in the probability of a defendant victory from each period to the next.[38] In each instance, the change is highly significant in both substantive and statistical terms. The probability of a pro-defendant decision in a typical case was .14 lower in 1981–84 than in the preceding period (standard error = .06). In 1985–92, the probability that the defendant would win increased by .21 (.05). It then decreased by .32 (.04) in the next period, 1993–2002, and jumped back up by .45 (.05) in the years after 2002. These are dramatic shifts.

The same dramatic shifts appear if we focus specifically on cases of explicit doctrinal change, that is, cases where the court overruled a precedent. To avoid including decisions to overrule obsolete cases, which would not reveal much about the direction of doctrinal movement on the court at a particular moment, we limit our analysis, somewhat arbitrarily, to overrulings of cases that were twenty-five years old or less.

Our search of Shepard's Citations did not yield a single overruling of a case up to twenty-five years old between 1973 and 1980. However, between 1981 and 1986 the court overruled fourteen such precedents in ten separate decisions. Another forty-five were overruled (in thirty-three cases) between 1987 and 2012. Of the fifty-nine total overrulings, forty-five favored plaintiffs and fourteen favored defendants.

The frequency and direction of overrulings varied considerably by period. All fourteen of the overrulings in the 1981–86 period moved the law in a more pro-plaintiff direction. Similarly, in the most concentrated period of change, from 1993 to 1996, all eighteen of the court's overrulings benefited plaintiffs. In contrast, between 2003 and 2012, only one overruling benefited plaintiffs, while six benefited defendants.

When we consider the court's membership, the timing of the shifts appears far from random. The vociferously pro-plaintiff Clifford Brown joined the court in 1981, and James Celebrezze came on in 1983, both replacing Republican justices. Celebrezze lost his reelection bid just two years later, and his brother Frank was defeated two years after that. The year 1993, the beginning of the next move left, was when pro-plaintiff Francis Sweeney took over the seat of pro-defendant Robert Holmes. Republican Deborah Cook replaced Democrat A. William Sweeney in 1995 and the pro-plaintiff swing was interrupted, but the bare liberal majority asserted itself in the next several years, until Andrew (Andy) Douglas left the bench and was replaced by Maureen O'Connor in 2003.[39] The pro-defendant consolidation continued with the replacements of Francis Sweeney with Judith Lanzinger in 2005 and of Alice Robie Resnick with Robert Cupp in 2007.

The court-level evidence for this account is entitled to be taken seriously. But it cannot be considered conclusive; it is possible that something—perhaps in the nature of the cases decided—caused sitting judges to change their behavior in ways that just happened to coincide with membership changes. For greater certainty we need to investigate the behavior of individual justices.

JUSTICES' VOTING BEHAVIOR

We begin by comparing the voting of consecutive occupants of the same seat on the court, excluding the three justices who each served only a few months to fill an unexpected vacancy (Robert Leach after C. William O'Neill's death, Eric Brown after Thomas Moyer's death, and David Dowd after Thomas Herbert's resignation). The first column of results in table 1.1 displays the change in proportion of votes for the defendant, moving from the earlier to later occupant of the seat. For instance, the first row tells us that Justice A. William Sweeney voted for defendants at a rate 19 percentage points lower than that of Justice John Corrigan, whom he replaced. With a standard error of only 5.6, the difference is highly significant. (Note that the figures for any justice are limited to cases decided by that justice between 1973 and 2012.)

The third column is a narrower comparison based on the court's term length of six years. It displays the difference between the voting of outgoing justices in their final six years and the voting of their successors in their first six years. (Fewer than six years are included where the justice's final term began before 1973, the justice's first term extended past 2012, or the justice served less than a full term on the court.) Looking again at the first row, we see that the shift from Corrigan to A. William Sweeney was far less momentous in the short term. (This is because Sweeney was much more pro-plaintiff in later years than in his first six.)[40]

The rest of the table reveals a striking amount of volatility. In a few cases the changes were small, especially where a justice replaced another from the same party (e.g., Cook to O'Donnell). However, far more often than not, the new justice favored defendants considerably more or less often than the justice he or she replaced. For analyses covering all years, eleven of the twenty changes were greater than 30 percentage points, and seven of those were greater than 40 percentage points. In the compari-

TABLE 1.1. Change in percentage of votes for tort defendants from departing justice to succeeding justice

JUSTICE PAIR (OLD→NEW)	CHANGE OVER ENTIRE PERIOD 1973–2012 (%)	STD. ERROR	CHANGE IN SIX (OR FEWER) YEARS BEFORE AND AFTER CHANGEOVER (%)	STD. ERROR
Corrigan→A. W. Sweeney (1977)	−19.0	5.6	−3.1	7.3
Stern→Locher (1977)	2.6	5.8	−3.0	7.0
O'Neill→Holmes (1978)	21.2	4.8	18.4	6.2
Herbert→C. Brown (1981)	−33.9	4.7	−30.2	5.4
P. Brown→Krupansky (1981)	24.7	7.8	24.9	8.1
Krupansky→J. Celebrezze (1983)	−63.0	7.2	−63.0	7.2
J. Celebrezze→Wright (1985)	48.9	5.2	53.3	5.4
W. Brown→Douglas (1985)	−14.9	3.4	−2.0	5.0
F. Celebrezze→Moyer (1987)	28.2	3.1	32.1	4.5
C. Brown→H. Brown (1987)	35.7	4.2	35.7	4.2
Locher→Resnick (1989)	−37.2	3.2	−33.3	4.6
Holmes→F. Sweeney (1993)	−54.4	3.0	−54.4	4.3
H. Brown→Pfeifer (1993)	−37.3	3.5	−35.1	4.7
A. W. Sweeney→Cook (1995)	40.6	3.8	50.4	4.6
Wright→Stratton (1996)	7.8	3.1	9.7	5.0
Douglas→O'Connor (2003)	43.5	3.7	38.9	3.0
Cook→O'Donnell (2003)	5.5	4.2	2.9	5.2
F. Sweeney→Lanzinger (2005)	46.2	4.2	44.9	5.3
Resnick→Cupp (2007)	46.4	4.5	50.1	5.7
Moyer→Y. Brown (2011)	−2.6	8.7	−3.3	9.7

Note: The second column is for all years a justice served between 1973 and 2012. The third column is for the final six (or fewer) years of the departing justice and first six (or fewer) years of the new justice.

sons of justices' last and first terms, there were twelve changes greater than 30 percent and six greater than 40 percent.

As striking as these numbers are, an important limitation to the data requires that they be treated with some caution. The two justices in each pair did not hear the same cases. As a result, we cannot be sure that the comparisons between justices are apt. For instance, it appears that Justice Holmes was a good deal more conservative than Chief Justice O'Neill. But perhaps defendants had stronger legal positions in the cases Justice Holmes heard, whether because the law had moved in a way that favored defendants, defendants were choosing their battles more wisely, the court was changing its own bases for accepting cases, or for some other reason. If so, then O'Neill might have voted for defendants more often if he had stayed on the bench. We cannot be sure how much the change from O'Neill to Holmes really benefited defendants.

In fact, we can imagine a scenario—unlikely but not impossible—where we would be compelled to reject the inference that Holmes was more predisposed toward defendants than O'Neill was. The six justices who served with O'Neill in the year and a half before his death were the same six who served with Holmes in his first year and a half on the bench. They ranged from strongly pro-plaintiff to strongly pro-defendant. Suppose that on examining the votes of all the justices, we found that O'Neill was usually in a minority of just one or two when he voted for the defendant but that Holmes was usually part of a comfortable majority in voting for the defendant. The most logical conclusion would be that Holmes was, if anything, *less* conservative relative to the continuing justices than O'Neill had been and that his apparently greater conservatism really reflected the fact that defendants brought much stronger cases to the court in his first two years on it than they had in the previous two.

Our statistical procedure for assessing and comparing the voting behavior of individual justices, while fairly complicated, always comes back to this logic. In other words, in estimating the impact of a new justice's arrival, we use information on the votes of other justices to take into account possible changes in the strength of defendants' cases that the court addressed before and after that arrival.

To illustrate our ultimate goal, the obstacles encountered, and our solutions for dealing with them, let us turn to the shift from Frank Celebrezze to Thomas Moyer in 1987. We know that Moyer favored the defendant considerably more often in the cases he heard than Celebrezze did in the cases he heard. But we do not know how large the difference between them would have been if they had been on the bench at the same time and decided the same cases. The challenge is to derive credible estimates of how Celebrezze would have voted in the cases Moyer heard if he had remained on the court.

We can generate such estimates by regressing Celebrezze's votes on measures of defendant case strength and then using the coefficients from that model and case-strength scores in later cases to predict how Celebrezze would have voted in those cases if he had been on the court. The ideal measure of the strength of the defendant's position would come directly from examination of the facts and law in each case. However, such a measure is not available to us; it would require both more information than we can readily acquire and excessive reliance on personal judgments. Fortunately, we have access to other valuable information that speaks to the strength of the defendant's case while requiring little in the way of coding judgments—namely, the votes of the other justices in the case.

The most straightforward vote-based measure of the strength of the defendant's case would be the proportion of other justices voting for the defendant. If the six justices other than Celebrezze all voted for the defendant, we might infer that the defendant's position was very strong; a 3-3 split would suggest a much closer case. The key drawback to this straightforward measure is that it fails to take into account the predispositions of the other judges. If those predispositions are fairly diverse and reasonably symmetrical, then inferences of this sort will rest on solid ground. But say that in reality all six of the other judges are strong conservatives; they might vote 6-0 in favor of the defendant even if the defendant's case is only decent, while a 3-3 split could actually indicate a very strong case for the plaintiff.

For this measure to be more useful, then, it needs to incorporate and reflect information about the other justices' leanings. Of course, we do not have excellent absolute measures of individual justices' preference for plaintiffs or defendants; if we did, the entire exercise we are describing would be unnecessary. What keeps this problem from being fatal is that absolute scores are unnecessary for determining what difference it made that one justice rather than another sat on the bench. That is, it is enough to say that one justice favored plaintiffs more often by 20 percentage points than the average member of the Ohio Supreme Court between 1973 and 2012. It is not important to be able to say how that judge would have compared to, say, a judge serving in Texas or California at the same time, much less a judge in Texas or California in 1943 or 2042. Accordingly, we improved the vote-based measure of defendant case strength in three steps.

To prepare for these steps, we coded each justice's vote in each case as 1 for pro-defendant, -1 for pro-plaintiff, and 0 for mixed. In the first step, we took the difference between that justice's vote score in a case and the mean vote score of all other justices who participated in the same case and then calculated the mean of that difference for all cases in that year. (We chose to let these means vary by year in recognition of the fact that justices' leanings can change over the course of their careers and as a way of controlling for the justices with whom they were being compared.) This yielded an *annual relative score* for each justice. The more pro-defendant the justice of interest was relative to the other six justices, the more positive this score was.

In the next step, we used these annual relative scores to weight each justice's contribution to the measure of strength of the defendant's case. Specifically, we subtracted the justice's annual relative score from the justice's vote in the case. To illustrate, Clifford Brown voted for the defendant considerably less often in 1983 (and every other year he was on the bench) than his fellow judges did. As a result, he received an annual relative score of -.61 that year. When it came to measuring defendant case strength in a 1983 case, a Clifford Brown vote for the defendant, rather than counting simply as 1, counted as 1 — (-.61), or 1.61. This reflects the fact that a vote by Brown for the defendant was especially strong evidence that the defendant had a good case. In contrast, because his voting for the plaintiff revealed little about whether the plaintiff really had the better case, it only counted as -1 — (-.61), or -.39, rather than a full -1. Similarly, pro-defendant votes by a justice with a strongly pro-defendant record are discounted, while pro-plaintiff votes by that judge receive extra weight.

In the final step, we added together these weighted votes for each participating justice (other than the justice of interest) and divided by the number of participating justices to generate the *mean weighted vote,* a measure of the strength of the defendant's position in each case.[41]

Returning to Frank Celebrezze, in the model predicting his vote in a given case, the measure of the strength of the defendant's case is the mean weighted vote of the justices other than Celebrezze who voted in that case. Note that the defendant-strength score for any given case is specific to each justice whose decision making is being modeled; there are seven different scores for each case. While suboptimal, this is necessary to avoid the circularity of having a judge's own vote count toward a measure of strength of case as presented to that judge.

We can then use the weighted votes for each tort case in which Celebrezze participated over his supreme court career in a logit model of his votes for or against the defendant; for purposes of the model, we disregard mixed votes.[42] Along with the weighted vote variable, we include two other independent variables to capture factors that might be expected to be related to defendant success—whether the defendant was the petitioner and whether the defendant was a government rather than a business. The results are shown in table 1.2.

Neither variable involving the identity of the defendant—whether

TABLE 1.2. Results of logistic regression analysis of votes in tort cases, Chief Justice Frank Celebrezze

VARIABLE	COEFFICIENT	STD. ERROR	SIGNIFICANCE
Weighted votes	2.71	.30	<.001
Defendant was petitioner	–.03	.17	.86
Defendant was government	–.278	.374	.46
Constant	–1.00	.22	<.001

Note: N = 345.

the defendant petitioned the court to hear the case or whether the defendant was a government—has a meaningful effect on Celebrezze's votes once the weighted votes of the other judges are taken into account. The weighted vote variable itself has a powerful effect. The sign of the constant indicates that Celebrezze is likely to vote for the plaintiff when the plaintiff's and defendant's cases are about equally strong, as measured by the weighted votes of his fellow judges. The sign of the weighted vote variable indicates that he becomes considerably more willing to vote for the defendant as the strength of the defendant's case grows.

Logit coefficients cannot be interpreted directly, but they can be used to generate the predicted probability of an outcome given particular values of the independent variables. If we set all three independent variables to zero, meaning the defendant was the respondent and was not a government and that the case was evenly balanced between the plaintiff's and defendant's sides, the probability that Celebrezze votes for the defendant is .27. If instead we simulate a case where the other judges fairly strongly favor the defendant by setting the weighted vote score one standard deviation above zero, the probability of a pro-defendant vote from Celebrezze increases to .72.

To estimate the probability that Celebrezze would have voted for the defendant in case X decided after he left the bench and was replaced by Moyer, we create an equation with the coefficients for each independent variable from table 1.2 and the values of those variables in case X, with the weighted vote score now excluding Moyer. Using that equation, we can estimate the probability that Celebrezze would have voted for the defendant. When we do this for all cases on which Moyer sat, there are a handful of cases where the estimated probability that Celebrezze would have voted for the defendant is quite high, many more where it is quite low. Overall, the mean predicted probability is .33; that is, our best guess is that Celebrezze would have voted for the defendant in a third of those cases if he had still been on the bench.

The method depicted in this example illustrates the basics of our approach, but it suffers from two shortcomings. First, the one-to-one comparison of justices is fully appropriate only where the departing judge lost a reelection bid to the incoming judge (as Celebrezze did to Moyer). If the departing judge resigned, retired, or died, as was the case for most of the departing judges in this study, there is no special reason for wanting to know how that particular judge would have voted in the future.

Second, predictive models with the specification shown in table 1.2 did not yield sufficiently accurate predictions for individual justices for us to have great confidence in them. When we used that model to predict Celebrezze's actual votes, for instance, the predicted proportions of pro-plaintiff and pro-defendant votes deviated somewhat from the actual proportions. Thus, while our estimated probability of .33 makes us feel quite sure that Celebrezze would have voted for the defendant substantially less than half the time in the cases Moyer heard, we are not prepared to give great credence to the specific estimate of .33.

We addressed both shortcomings by changing one key part of the procedure. Instead of comparing the votes of the new judge to the hypothetical votes of the judge replaced, we compared them to the hypothetical votes of a typical judge from the other side of the ideological aisle. Not only is this a meaningful comparison in all circumstances, but the inclusion of far more justice votes in the prediction model allows us to make more confident estimates of the hypothetical behavior.

For example, Resnick attained her seat in an open-seat contest in 1988. Her predecessor, Locher, was barred by age from running again. Ideally, we would be able to imagine how the candidate defeated by Resnick, Joyce George, would have voted had she won, but we have no individualized basis for doing so. Instead, we can operate on the reasonable assumption that George would have voted about as the typical pro-defendant judge would.

For the most part, Democratic justices in this period favored plaintiffs more than Republican justices did. However, two of the most strongly and importantly pro-plaintiff judges, Douglas and Pfeifer, were Republicans. Rather than ignore this obvious fact, we include them with the Democrats when generating estimates for the typical justice on the more pro-plaintiff side.

To further strengthen the model for estimating justices' proportions of pro-defendant votes, we investigated several variants of the initial model and assessed them on the basis of their success in predicting actual justices' votes; we will discuss that prediction process shortly. The most successful predictive model to emerge from our testing was a simple one. In addition to the weighted vote score explained earlier, it includes an unweighted vote score—that is, the proportion of other justices favoring the defendant. It is not entirely clear to us why including both measures works better, except that each, obviously, is picking up something that the other misses. In any case, since our aim in the model is not to explain justices' votes but to predict them, the model with more accurate predictions is the better choice.

As an illustration of our testing method and the power of the final model, consider the voting of A. William Sweeney and Craig Wright. The mean support rate for defendants among all Democratic justices plus Douglas and Pfeifer was .332. The rate for Sweeney was .340, making him an excellent example of a typical pro-plaintiff justice. The mean support rate for all the Republican justices excluding Douglas and Pfeifer was .696. Wright's rate was .703, so he serves well as an example of a typical pro-defendant judge. A good test of whether a model can yield accurate trustworthy predictions of the voting behavior of a hypothetical typical judge is whether it can yield accurate predictions of an actual typical judge.

If we pool the votes of all the justices except Wright, regress them (using logit) on the two vote scores (one weighted, one unweighted) and a dummy variable for Democrat, Pfeifer, or Douglas (1) versus Republican (0), and then use the results to predict how a typical pro-defendant justice would have voted in the cases Wright sat on, we get a mean predicted support rate of .688, quite close to his actual rate of .703. Doing the same for Sweeney yields an even closer correspondence—a mean predicted rate of .3397 as compared with his actual rate of .3396. In other words, our method for estimating the likely votes of a typical justice on one side or the other generates highly credible estimates, and meaningful comparisons between actual and hypothetical justices can be made with them.

Table 1.3 displays this comparison for every justice who joined the Ohio Supreme Court after 1973. That is, it shows (1) the actual proportion of pro-defendant votes cast by that justice and (2) the model estimate for the proportion of pro-defendant votes that would have been cast by a typical justice from the other party (or, for Douglas and Pfeifer, from the other ideological side) in those same cases. It does this twice:

TABLE 1.3. Comparisons of justices' pro-defendant votes with estimated votes of a typical justice on the other side

	ENTIRE PERIOD 1973–2012 (%)		FIRST SIX YEARS ONLY (%)	
JUSTICE	ACTUAL	COUNTERFACTUAL	ACTUAL	COUNTERFACTUAL
A. W. Sweeney (D)	34.0	65.6	50.0	68.5
Locher (D)	63.5	68.7	57.8	69.3
Holmes (R)	75.8	38.6	72.5	35.6
C. Brown (D)	22.0	63.9	same	
Krupansky (R)	84.4	34.1	same	
J. Celebrezze (D)	21.4	60.2	same	
Wright (R)	70.3	37.1	74.8	41.5
Douglas (R)	27.7	65.8	41.5	70.2
Moyer (R)	64.3	34.2	68.7	38.8
H. Brown (D)	57.3	69.3	same	
Resnick (D)	26.3	65.3	32.9	64.2
F. Sweeney (D)	21.4	64.0	21.2	62.2
Pfeifer (R)	20.0	66.3	22.2	61.4
Cook (R)	74.7	30.5	77.1	31.1
Stratton (R)	78.1	37.2	75.8	27.8
O'Connor (R)	71.2	42.8	73.7	41.9
O'Donnell (R)	80.3	45.0	80.2	43.9
Lanzinger (R)	67.7	43.4	66.7	42.1
Cupp (R)	72.7	46.2	same	
Y. Brown (D)	61.7	71.7	same	

Notes: "Actual" is the justice's percentage of votes in favor of tort defendants. "Counterfactual" is, except in the cases of Douglas and Pfeifer, the percentage of votes for the defendant that the model estimates would have been cast by a typical member of the other party in the same cases. For Douglas and Pfeifer, the comparison is to a typical Republican.

for the justice's entire career (shown in the first two columns of results) and, if that justice served more than one six-year term, for the justice's first term only (shown in the last two columns).

Table 1.4 translates these predictions into estimates of net votes won or lost by defendants because a given justice, rather than a typical justice from the other side, sat on the cases. Estimates in the first column of results (net vote for defendants, all cases) are generated in three steps. First, we estimate the number of pro-plaintiff votes by the actual justice that would have been cast for the defendant if the hypothetical judge had been sitting instead by multiplying the total pro-plaintiff votes of the actual justice by the mean predicted probability of a pro-defendant vote by a judge from the other side in that set of cases. For instance, if Justice X

TABLE 1.4. Difference between actual pro-defendant votes and estimated votes of a typical justice on the other side

JUSTICE	YEARS ON THE COURT	NET VOTES FOR DEFENDANT: ALL CASES	NET VOTES FOR DEFENDANT: CASES WITH A MINIMUM WINNING COALITION
A. W. Sweeney (D)	18	−170	−38
Locher (D)	12	−16	−8
Holmes (R)	14	+167	+30
C. Brown (D)	6	−101	−25
Krupansky (R)	3	+23	+3
J. Celebrezze (D)	2	−32	−6
Wright (R)	11	+125	+27
Douglas (R)	18	−200	−72
Moyer (R)	23	+170	+39
H. Brown (D)	6	−19	−6
Resnick (D)	18	−159	−55
F. Sweeney (D)	12	−122	−51
Pfeifer (R)	20	−206	−55
Cook (R)	8	+82	+12
Stratton (R)	17	+133	+21
O'Donnell (R)	9	+60	+12
O'Connor (R)	10	+50	+13
Lanzinger (R)	8	+35	+4
Cupp (R)	6	+30	+3
Y. Brown (D)	2	−3	−1

voted for the plaintiff 100 times, and the mean of the counterfactual predictions is .82, our best guess is that a judge from the other side would have supported the plaintiff only 18 out of those 100 times, making a net loss to defendants of 82 votes that they otherwise would have received. Second, we do the same thing for pro-defendant votes by multiplying the total pro-defendant votes of the actual justice by the mean estimated probability of a pro-plaintiff vote (i.e., 1.0 minus the estimated probability of a pro-defendant vote) by a judge on the other side. Suppose Justice X voted for defendants 20 times, and the mean counterfactual predicted probability of a pro-plaintiff vote in those cases was 0.1. Our best guess is that 2 of those 20 votes would have gone to the defendant in our counterfactual world.

The third step is subtracting the first product from the second: 2 − 82 = -80, meaning that defendants received 80 fewer votes across Justice X's career than they would have if a judge from the other side had occupied that seat instead.

To get a better sense of how these votes might have affected outcomes, we can focus specifically on majority votes in cases decided by a minimum winning coalition, where a change in any one vote on the majority side would also change the outcome. Results for these votes, using the method just described, appear in the second column of results in table 1.4. We would remind readers that these numbers should not be taken too literally. They are only estimates, and they undoubtedly contain substantial error. However, even considered with due caution the picture they paint is again striking, suggesting that hundreds of cases in this period would have been decided differently if individual elections had come out differently.

At the individual level, Douglas appears to have been the most consequential justice; we estimate that 72 cases would have been decided for defendants rather than plaintiffs if a typical Republican had occupied his seat instead. Francis Sweeney matches him if we consider influence in annual terms; both averaged about 4 cases per year that would have been decided the other way with a typical Republican in his place. Moyer was the most consequential pro-defendant Republican across an entire career, though Holmes and Wright affected more outcomes per year. The individual differences reflect not only the justices' voting behavior, but also the environments in which they served. For instance, although the estimated number of pro-plaintiff votes that can be credited to (or blamed on) Pfeifer (206) is slightly higher than the number for Douglas (200), Pfeifer appears to have affected fewer outcomes. This undoubtedly is because more of his career was spent on a court dominated by one side (specifically, by pro-defendant justices), where his pro-plaintiff votes could not change the outcome.

These estimates of probabilities are telling, suggesting that virtually every election over the forty-year period had consequences for the level of support for plaintiffs and defendants on the Ohio Supreme Court. With some caution, we can also use the model to make statements about individual cases.

Recall the court's decisions in the mid-1980s to abolish parental and spousal immunity. Clifford Brown voted with the 4-3 majority in both cases. The model's counterfactual prediction for his vote in the former case—that is, our estimate of the probability that a typical Republican in Brown's case would have voted the other way—is .81. For the spousal immunity case, the estimate is .86. We can feel fairly certain that at least one of these cases would have been decided the other way had a typical Republican been on the bench rather than Brown.

Or we might ask how likely it is that the court in 1991 would have upheld, rather than struck down, the statute limiting suits against employers for intentional torts if business groups had been able to unseat A. William Sweeney and replace him with a typical Republican justice. The counterfactual estimate of .78 suggests that there is a better than three out of four chance that the statute would have survived.

One of the court's most important pro-defendant decisions—followed by Ohio courts 328 times since 2003, according to Shepard's Citations—was *Westfield Insurance Co. v. Galatis.*[43] *Galatis* involved the recurring issue of uninsured motorist coverage and the strangely persistent insurers' practice of including "you" as a covered class in auto policies issued to corporations. As the court had pointed out in a 1999 decision, a corporation, being unable to drive—or even fit into—a car, could not very well suffer a physical injury in one.[44] The term *you* was, therefore, ambiguous as applied to a corporation in an uninsured motorist clause; it must either mean nothing or refer to employees of the corporation. Opting for the latter reading, the court had ruled in favor of an off-duty employee who, while driving his wife's car, was injured by an uninsured driver. *Galatis* partially overruled this decision, holding that employees are covered by such policies only when acting within the scope of their employment.

Justice O'Connor wrote the opinion for the 4-3 majority in *Galatis.* Had a typical Democrat heard that case in O'Connor's stead, the probability that the outcome would have been the same—by our best estimate—is only .12.

OVERRULING CASES

As telling as these analyses of counterfactual votes are, they do rely on inference. For more direct, albeit more limited, information about the relationship between membership change and policy change in the court, we can examine decisions to overrule precedents.

Recall that the court overruled fifty-nine cases that were twenty-five years old or less between 1981 and 2012. We can assess the impact of membership change by focusing on those instances where the position of a given seat on the court was in the majority in both the precedential case and the decision overruling it—for instance, where Justice O'Connor voted to overrule a precedent that her predecessor, Justice Douglas, had voted for when he was on the court.

In a fair number of cases where the vote from a given seat on the court changed, justices voted to overrule themselves. (Remarkably, A. William Sweeney did this eight times, seven of which saw him move in a pro-plaintiff direction.) Excluding these leaves us with 136 instances.

Not every one resembles the example of O'Connor's overruling of Douglas, with a judge from one side of the ideological aisle voting in the expected direction to overrule a precedent supported by a judge from the other side. On eighteen occasions the direction of movement was the opposite of what one would expect—for example, Chief Justice Moyer twice voted to overrule pro-defendant decisions that had been supported by Chief Justice Celebrezze. Nevertheless, there are numerous instances—118, to be precise—of a justice voting in the expected direction to undo the vote of another justice. In 102 of those precedents, the overruled vote was cast by a justice from the other side of the ideological aisle. (In the remaining sixteen, the judge who cast the earlier vote was a visiting judge or a justice from the overruling justice's ideological camp.)

Table 1.5 summarizes the overruling behavior of all justices who were part of an overruling majority more than twice. The column of results shows the number of successful overruling votes in the expected ideo-

TABLE 1.5. Successful votes to overrule tort precedents, selected justices

JUSTICE	OVERRULED PREDECESSORS	NUMBER OF CASES
C. Brown	Herbert	8 (0)
J. Celebrezze	P. Brown/Krupansky	5 (0)
Douglas	W. Brown	12 (2)
Wright	P. Brown/Krupansky/J. Celebrezze	5 (4)
Moyer	F. Celebrezze	5 (3)
H. Brown	Herbert/C. Brown	7 (1)
Resnick	Stern/Locher	20 (0)
F. Sweeney	Holmes	23 (0)
Pfeifer	Herbert/C.Brown/H. Brown	15 (0)
Stratton	Wright	1 (2)
O'Connor	Douglas	6 (1)
O'Donnell	A. W. Sweeney	3 (1)
Cupp	Locher/Resnick	4 (1)

Notes: Justices included here are those who voted to overrule precedents at least twice in cases in which the court did overrule those precedents. The overruled predecessors are justices who had held the same seat and who had voted for one or more of the overruled precedents. In the last column, the first number is the number of overruling votes consistent with the justice's normal voting pattern; the number in parentheses is the number of overruling votes contrary to the justice's normal voting pattern.

logical direction and, in parentheses, the number of overruling votes that went contrary to that justice's normal pattern. The champion overruler was Francis Sweeney, who voted with the majority to overrule twenty-three pro-defendant decisions, twenty-two of which had been joined by his immediate predecessor, Holmes. Resnick voted to overrule nearly as often. Usually her target was Locher, but in several instances the overruled case had been decided while she was a member of the court but not participating. The most important justice for the defendants' side was Herbert Brown, who seven times contributed to overruling pro-plaintiff precedents supported by his immediate predecessor, Clifford Brown.

EFFECTS ON SITTING JUSTICES

It is clear that judicial elections influenced the development of tort law in Ohio by altering the composition of the court. Of course, elections can also influence policy by creating a threatening environment that encourages sitting elected officials to alter their behavior in the hope of retaining their seats at the next election (Stimson, Mackuen, and Erikson 1995). As discussed in the introduction, there is some evidence that the prospect of elections has that effect on elected judges. Did supreme court elections play that role in torts in Ohio?

Extensive analyses, which, because of their complexity, we will discuss only in summary, suggest that the answer is most likely no. We cannot rule out the possibility that individual justices, looking over their shoulders, occasionally cast different votes than they would have in a different electoral environment. But the overall pattern of evidence offers no solid ground for attributing the court's major shifts in doctrine and case outcomes to the responsiveness of continuing justices.

The first stage of our analytical strategy was to look for evidence of environment-sensitive decision making where it would most likely be found, by comparing justices who had reason to worry about elections with those who did not. Recall that, like most other states, Ohio imposes age limits on its judges: once they reach seventy, they can finish the term they are serving but are not eligible to serve another. By definition, justices who are not eligible for reelection can have no incentive to modify their behavior in an effort to earn interest groups' electoral support or forestall the active opposition of other groups. If the electoral environment affected justices' decision making, we should see systematic differences between the votes of justices who were eligible for reelection and the votes of justices who were not.

We do not. A long series of analyses involving varying sets of justices and combinations of control variables yielded no consistent evidence that all justices, pro-plaintiff justices alone, or pro-defendant justices alone tended in one direction or the other when eligible for reelection.[45]

It might be that this approach is too crude. Eligible officials might modify their behavior more toward the ends of their terms, reasoning that decisions made earlier in their terms are likely to be forgotten by the time the next election comes (Thomas 1985; Bernhard and Sala 2006). Evidence of such behavior in the criminal law domain has been found in several studies of elected judges (e.g., M. G. Hall 1995; Huber and Gordon 2004; Gordon and Huber 2007). However, we did not find it in Ohio. We compared justices' voting in the last two years of an eligible term with their voting in all other years. Neither in pooled analyses nor in individual analyses of justices were there any indications that justices became more or less pro-defendant as a reelection campaign approached.

The second stage of our strategy was simply to examine variations across each justice's career in support for defendants. There were some changes: Justices Locher and Wright became somewhat more conservative later in their careers and A. William Sweeney became more liberal, Justices Resnick and Douglas became more liberal after their first two or three years on the bench, and Chief Justice Moyer also appeared to move to the left, relative to the other justices. (We think his apparent movement is at least partly explained by the accession of Republican justices who were more consistently pro-defendant than he was.) But the other justices showed little or no clear movement, and to the extent there was movement, we could not detect any telling commonality across justices. That is, no larger pattern is discernible. And what movement there is does not track doctrinal developments on the court in any evident way. In short, we see no basis for inferring that judicial responsiveness to the electoral environment explains the doctrinal and decisional variation documented in this chapter.

Looking Ahead

The lesson of the chapter, then, is that judicial elections had a tremendous effect on Ohio tort law between 1973 and 2012 and that they did so by changing the court's composition. Seats changed hands between pro-plaintiff and pro-defendant justices with remarkable frequency, and the court's membership changes often produced marked shifts in doctrine and in parties' win rates.

The next two chapters probe the roles of interest groups and voters in bringing about these changes. In chapter 2 we examine the extent to which groups responded to stakes and opportunities they perceived in election contests, pouring money and energy into some and largely ignoring others. We also analyze media coverage to describe the visibility and main public themes of various contests.

Chapter 3 asks how voters responded when groups upped their spending and activity. Specifically, we try to determine how much influence group spending and activity had over election outcomes and how well voters understood and welcomed the part they themselves played in shaping Ohio tort law.

TWO

Campaigns and Elections

In the preceding chapter, we documented how the Ohio Supreme Court's rulings on tort policies evolved over time, largely as a result of membership replacement. In a situation of member-driven policy change, interest groups that care about issues before the court may mobilize either to elect candidates who will move the court in their preferred direction or to protect incumbents who support their positions. They can do so in numerous ways, including endorsing candidates, contributing to their campaigns or political parties, and spending money independently of the campaigns on advertisements and mailers. They may focus their efforts directly on their issue of concern (e.g., workers' compensation) or instead protect their interests indirectly by drawing voters' attention to such issues as judges' ideologies and experience or their votes in criminal cases.

In this chapter, we trace the history of supreme court campaigns in Ohio, dividing the elections into five eras and illustrating when and how interest groups became heavily engaged in the elections. The interest groups of particular interest to us are business groups and their allies on the side of tort defendants and labor unions and trial lawyers on the side of tort plaintiffs.[1] For convenience, we will refer to the two sides as "business" and "pro-plaintiff." Looking beyond Ohio, we develop and probe some theoretical explanations for when interest groups become most active in campaigns, and our history provides an important reminder that, even in an age of much more visible judicial contests, not all judicial campaigns are equally visible or equally important. Because the broader theoretical framework will be helpful for structuring and understanding our narrative, we turn to that first, before delving into the recent history of Ohio Supreme Court election campaigns.

Predicting Group Activity and Involvement

When Justice at Stake and its partner groups first released the report *New Politics of Judicial Elections,* discussed in the introduction, the subtitle—*How 2000 Was a Watershed Year for Big Money, Special Interest Pressure, and TV Advertising in State Supreme Court Campaigns*—might have led one to believe that the rising costs of judicial elections, increased negativity, and engagement by interest groups and political parties were features of all supreme court elections.

However, reading the report makes it clear that not all supreme court elections are high-profile contests. In fact, some still look very much like the stereotypical judicial elections of old—sleepy affairs with little outside involvement and not much at stake. For example, while thirteen supreme court candidates in Alabama combined to raise more than $13 million in 2000, fourteen candidates in Washington State spent a little under $1 million combined (Goldberg et al. 2002, 11).

What accounts for this variation? One possible answer is the selection method for justices. Since partisan elections are overtly political, candidates and parties may feel more at liberty to raise money. Further, partisan contests tend to be more competitive than those conducted with a nonpartisan ballot (M. G. Hall and Bonneau 2006; Bonneau 2005).

There does seem to be some evidence to support this proposition in that supreme court elections in partisan states like Alabama, Illinois, Mississippi, and West Virginia (before that state moved to a nonpartisan ballot for supreme court races in 2015) have often been the most expensive, contentious, and visible, with substantial involvement from outside groups (see Goldberg et al. 2002). To return to the earlier example, Alabama's supreme court elections are partisan, while those in Washington are nonpartisan.

However, the partisan ballot cannot explain all of the variation in campaigns. First, there is evidence that parties and interest groups are active and influential in nonpartisan judicial contests (Goldberg 2007; Streb 2007) and retention elections (M. G. Hall 2001; Streb 2015, 51). Second, and perhaps more important, great variation in visibility and group involvement often exists within a state where ballot type does not vary.

Ohio is a perfect illustration of this phenomenon. Figures 2.1, 2.2, and 2.3 show the amount of news coverage, campaign contributions, and television advertising in Ohio Supreme Court races.[2] It is clear from all

FIGURE 2.1. Number of newspaper articles covering Ohio Supreme Court elections in the *Columbus Dispatch*, 1986–2012

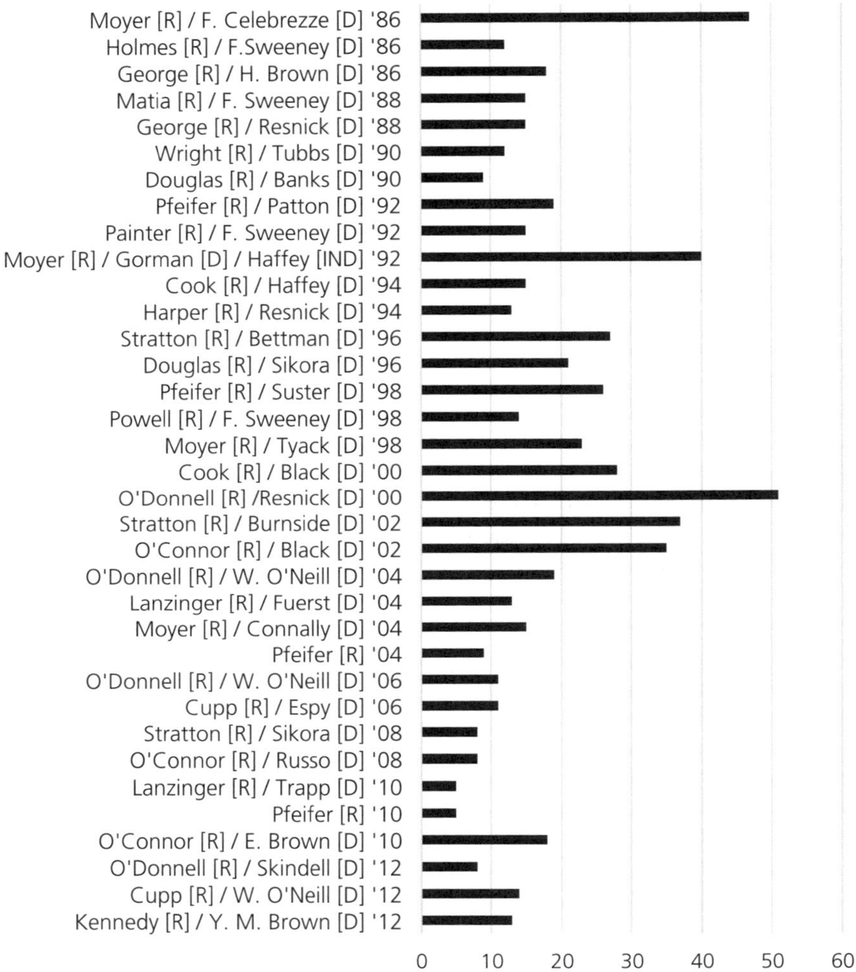

Source: Newsbank file of articles in the *Columbus Dispatch*.

three figures that some races are more visible than others. In some years, voters were able to read many articles about the contest and were highly likely to view television commercials (see, e.g., the 2000 supreme court elections). In other years (e.g., 2012) the news media essentially ignored the races, and candidates raised minimal contributions because interest groups were not engaged, making it difficult to advertise on television. And it is not solely the change in political context in different years that

FIGURE 2.2. Total contributions to Ohio Supreme Court candidates, 1992–2012, adjusted for inflation (2012 dollars)

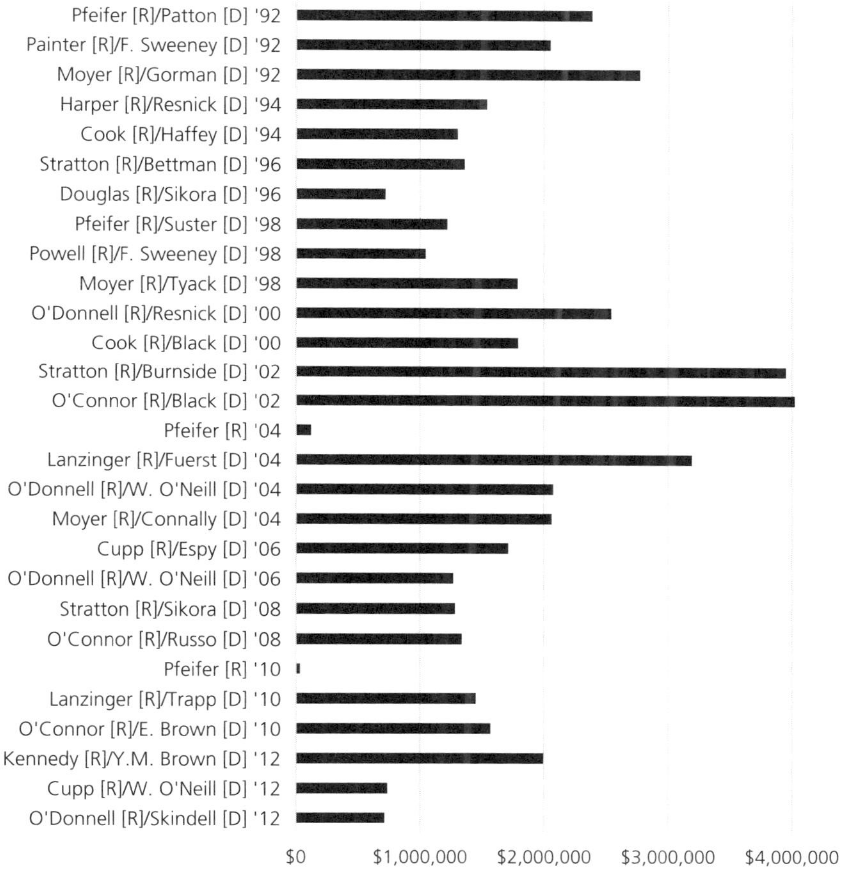

Source: National Institute on Money in State Politics (http://www.followthemoney.org/).

causes the variation. Even within the same year, differences in visibility can exist. For example, the 2000 contest between Alice Robie Resnick and Terrence O'Donnell received far more newspaper coverage and there was far more spending on television ads in their contest than in the race between Tim Black and Deborah Cook in the same year.

The question then is why some supreme court elections resemble races for the US Senate while others have more in common with elections for obscure local offices. We think the best—though still necessarily incomplete—answer begins with a consideration of stakes and

FIGURE 2.3. Total cost and number of airings of television advertisements in Ohio Supreme Court elections, 2000–2012

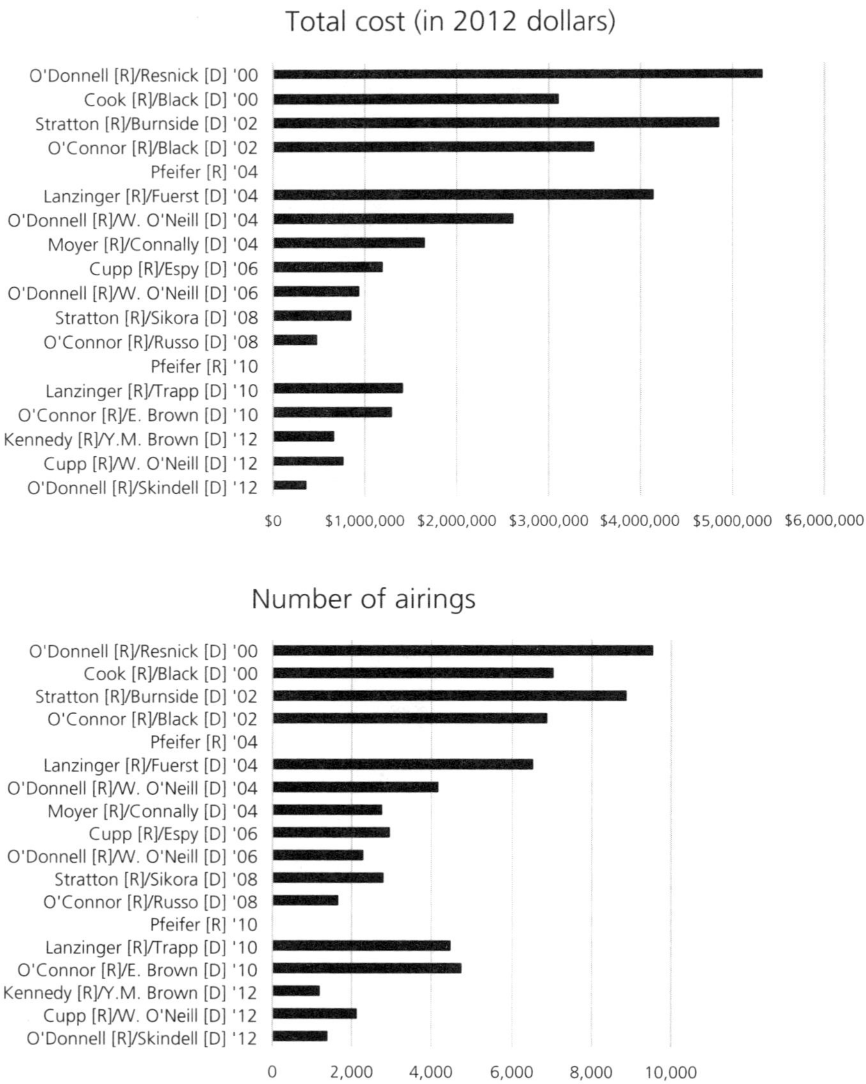

Source: Justice at Stake (and partner groups), *New Politics of Judicial Elections* reports, 2000–2012 (www.justiceatstake.org/resources/the_new_politics_of_judicial_elections.cfm).

competitiveness. Interest group activity should be greater when there is much at stake in the court's decisions and where one set of interests has a realistic chance of adding a sympathetic judge to the bench, less when the stakes are low or where one side has little chance of wresting a seat from the other.

What is perceived to be at stake may be a function of numerous factors. Undoubtedly one of the most important is a court's recent rulings. As discussed in the introduction, the relationship here is more complex than that interest groups get involved when the court makes an unwelcome ruling. Some decisions are more far-reaching than others. One minor ruling might annoy a group but not spur it to take action. However, a major ruling, such as one that eliminated medical malpractice caps, might by itself be enough to get interest groups involved. And a series of minor rulings in opposition to the group's interest could have a cumulative effect that sparks involvement. If, for example, a court issued a series of modest decisions favoring claims for uninsured motorist coverage, the insurance community would likely mobilize to shift the court in a different direction. Although the comparison is not perfect, there is evidence that interest groups are more engaged in legislative campaigns when legislatures have passed laws that run counter to the groups' positions (Jacobson 1999).

Interest groups are reactive in this account, but we should not be surprised if groups look ahead as well. If a major case or set of cases is pending before the court, groups will likely work to elect a court favorable to their interests. Even in the absence of major pending cases, groups may have strong incentives to seek a court whose overall pattern of decisions will be favorable to their interests. Presumably perceptions of the court's recent activity and coming cases play into each other, so that the stakes seem greatest when important cases are on the horizon and the court has demonstrated a willingness to make major pronouncements or a strong tendency to favor one side.

The stakes in an election will be especially high when the contest is to fill a swing seat—that is, when the outcome of an election may shift the majority from one side to the other and potentially move the court in an entirely different direction. It is common in legislative elections for more attention to be focused on certain races that can change the majority in the body; this tendency should be even more pronounced in races for a supreme court, as there are fewer people needed to change the direction of a court. When the court is closely divided, interest group activity should increase because much is at stake.

All else being equal, then, interest groups should be most active when the court has recently handed down major decisions or adopted a general position that is unfavorable to the groups' interests, when groups anticipate future decisions that are important to those interests, and when the majority of the court is up for grabs in the upcoming election. All else may not be equal, however. Suppose all these conditions hold but the seat to be contested is held by a popular incumbent and the other side cannot find a credible candidate to challenge him or her. We would not expect rational groups on either side to expend much effort or money if the outcome of the election appears to be a foregone conclusion. By the same token, if groups spot a particularly good chance to capture a seat from the other side, especially a seat that would give them a majority on the court, they might pour resources into it even in the absence of recent or upcoming cases of great importance, knowing that such cases are bound to arise sometime. So the competitiveness of the race may influence the level of interest group activity.

The single most important predictor of competitiveness is whether the race is for an open seat. The incumbency advantage has been well documented for most elected offices in the United States (see, e.g., Jacobson and Carson 2015; Herrnson 2011; Jewell and Cassie 1998). This advantage exists for many reasons. Incumbents have a record on which to run and can point to popular positions that they have taken in favor of their constituents; challengers may not have that ability. Because incumbents have access to a network of donors who have supported them in the past (Jacobson and Carson 2015; Herrnson 2011), they generally raise more money than challengers, making it easier to promote their campaign's message to voters. And incumbents often simply have greater name recognition than challengers, which may be enough to convince people to vote for them (Jacobson and Carson 2015; Schaffner, Streb, and Wright 2001).

As a result, a nonincumbent has a much greater probability of winning when no incumbent is on the ballot (Jacobson and Carson 2015; Bonneau 2006; Gaddie and Bullock 2000). Potential challengers know this, so open seats are more likely to attract the highest quality challengers, and those challengers in turn are more likely to receive support from groups who have something at stake in the outcome of the election (Jacobson 1989; Mondak 1995; Stone, Maisel, and Maestas 2004). The result of all this is that the presence or absence of an incumbent in a race is one of the best predictors of a contest's visibility and competitiveness (Jacobson and Kernell 1983; Abramowitz and Segal 1992; Gaddie and Bullock 2000; Jacobson and Carson 2015; Hogan 2000).

The incumbency advantage in judicial elections is more complex. Judges certainly have a record on which to run, but it is not common for judges to publicize decisions they have reached. One reason may be a feeling that it is inappropriate to talk even about cases that have already been resolved. Moreover, the opportunity to perform casework—work on behalf of constituents to help solve a problem with government—does not exist for judges. Because of the low visibility of state supreme courts, one might expect incumbent judges to benefit even more from name recognition. Yet, most justices are unknown to the public. In fact, one poll about the Ohio Supreme Court found that only 4 percent of Ohioans could name a justice on the highest court in the state.[3]

Even if the nature of the incumbency advantage is not the same for supreme court justices as it is for other elected officials, it still exists. Incumbent justices are far more likely to win than lose, no matter what the election method—though they do better in nonpartisan contests (Bonneau 2005; M. G. Hall 2001, 2007; Streb, Frederick, and LaFrance 2007; Kritzer 2015, 113–20). In the six states in which incumbency is listed on the ballot (Ohio does not list incumbency), that designation might be advantageous (but see Klein and Baum 2001, 716–17).

The ballot aside, it is quite possible that the incumbent benefits from name recognition. The statistic mentioned about knowledge of Ohio Supreme Court justices concerned people's ability to *recall* the names of justices. This is different from *recognizing* the names on a ballot. People may not be able to remember the name of the candidate for whom they are voting when they enter the voting booth, but they may cast their ballot for that candidate once they see a name that looks familiar. Indeed, news coverage of incumbent justices is usually greater than news coverage of nonincumbents (see table 2.1), which makes it more likely that voters will be able to recognize incumbents as opposed to challengers. Because the odds of defeating a sitting justice are low, interest groups may shy away from supporting their challengers.

Incumbency is not the only determinant of competitiveness, however, and not all incumbents are safe. In fact, some can be quite vulnerable for a variety of reasons. They may be in the midst of a scandal, have a divisive personality, or have made controversial rulings that can effectively be turned against them in campaign ads. Even if incumbents are themselves strong candidates, the political context is constantly chang-

TABLE 2.1. Number of stories mentioning incumbent and nonincumbent candidates for the same seat for selected races

	DISPATCH		*PLAIN DEALER*		
	INCUMBENT	CHALLENGER	INCUMBENT	CHALLENGER	CANDIDATES
1988	71	40			A. W. Sweeney-Matia
1990	64	18			Douglas-Banks
1994	69	24	50	21	Resnick-Harper
1998	121	39	77	24	Moyer-Tyack
2000	84	42	49	37	Cook-Black
2002	110	62	89	67	Stratton-Burnside

Source: Newsbank files of articles in the *Columbus Dispatch* and the *Cleveland Plain Dealer.*
Note: Races where incumbents had significant negative coverage (e.g., Celebrezze in 1986; Resnick in 2000) and races where candidates had common last names for Ohio Supreme Court candidates (e.g., Brown, O'Neill) are not included. In the "Candidates" column, the incumbent is listed first.

ing, and national or state trends may work against them. A strong year for Republicans nationally or statewide, for example, could trickle down to affect Democratic supreme court candidates' chances for success. Empirical evidence exists that state legislative candidates benefit from the coattails of a governor from the same party (Hogan 2005); it is probable that the same phenomenon occurs in judicial elections, at least in states that use a partisan ballot.

Groups attempting to gauge an incumbent's vulnerability will likely pay close attention to how well the incumbent performed in the last election (M. G. Hall and Bonneau 2006). They will also take note of whether the incumbent was appointed as a replacement and has yet to run in an election (Bonneau 2005; M. G. Hall and Bonneau 2006).[4] Incumbents who narrowly won their last election or have not faced the voters yet may not have solid reelection constituencies, making them ripe for defeat.

The effects of these vulnerabilities may be magnified by strategic challengers. Research on congressional and state legislative races (Mondak 1995; Stone, Maisel, and Maestas 2004; Van Dunk 1997; Hogan 2004) and judicial elections (M. G. Hall and Bonneau 2006; Streb and Frederick 2009) finds that potential challengers act strategically, carefully appraising the characteristics of sitting officeholders and gauging the likelihood of defeating them before deciding whether to take them on. Assuming that stronger challengers are more likely to take a shot when

their chances of winning are better, their emergence will make campaigns against vulnerable incumbents even more attractive to interest groups.

In sum, predicting interest group activity can be thought of in this way: interest groups are most apt to be involved when the court has shifted policy or appears likely to do so, when control of the court is at stake, and when the seat is open or held by a vulnerable incumbent. The elections with the greatest amount of interest group involvement should be those where two or more of these factors appear together. Interest group activity should be minimal in instances where no policy shift has taken place or seems likely to take place, the majority is not at stake, and there is an incumbent who is not vulnerable.

However, we do not mean to overstate the predictive power of these attributes of supreme court contests. For one thing, interest group decisions are based on their leaders' perceptions of the reality relating to particular contests. While perceptions of the stakes in a contest are likely to match the reality well, perceptions of the competitiveness of a contest can be inaccurate, especially because of the limited amount of polling that is usually conducted for supreme court races. Indeed, we will discuss some contests that had surprising outcomes or that were closer or more one-sided than expected.

Further, groups can expend only the resources that are available for use in supreme court contests. On the pro-plaintiff side, the weakening of the labor movement may have limited its financial involvement in supreme court contests, especially when the movement had other political commitments in a given election year.

Finally, there is always the possibility of idiosyncratic choices. The perspectives of particular leaders and internal politics, for instance, may shape interest group strategies. For this reason, no model of interest group decisions can fully explain the level of group involvement in electoral contests.

Interest Group Involvement during Various Eras of the Ohio Supreme Court

To examine interest group activity and other attributes of Ohio Supreme Court elections, we rely on newspaper accounts, campaign contribution and spending reports, and campaign advertisements.[5] Unfortunately, we do not have complete information for all elections. Information on newspaper coverage of campaigns and on contributions to campaigns and spending by candidates is more readily available beginning in the 1990s than in earlier periods.[6] Information on television commercial transcripts and ad buys is presented in various degrees of detail in the successive *New Politics* reports of Justice at Stake and associated groups, and these provide a clearer picture of the strategies used by candidates, parties, and other organizations. However, those data are only available back to 2000. Political parties and interest groups have spent significant sums of money in some supreme court contests at least as far back as 1996. But unlike contributions to candidates and expenditures by those candidates, those sums do not have to be reported to the Secretary of State's office (or to anyone else); the only information we have about that spending comes from the spending figures for television ads in the *New Politics* reports since 2000. It is also important to note that we view these elections as outside observers and through a retrospective lens. We were not on the inside as these campaigns were being conducted and so we are forced to rely primarily on how the campaigns were covered in the media.

Nevertheless, the information that is available provides valuable background for understanding the campaigns, especially their visibility and interest group involvement. The descriptive discussion in this chapter sets the stage for the empirical analyses in the next chapter related to participation and voting. Understanding when campaigns had substantial interest group involvement and what the strategies were during those campaigns will allow us to assess the impact they had on potential voters, in terms of both participation and vote choice.

We divide the history of Ohio Supreme Court elections into five eras. We provide a narrative for each, focusing primarily on two aspects. First, we address how much groups participated in different eras (and specific contests) and why. Second, we focus on what the campaigns were about and how they were covered. Note that these eras do not coincide with those we analyzed in chapter 1 because they reflect patterns of campaign activity rather than court policies. As we will show, interest groups become involved primarily when the conditions discussed above (recent rulings, vulnerable incumbent, and so on) existed. Because of the limited information available for the first era and the large amount of time it covers, we simply provide an overview of the era to help set the stage for what was to come.

QUIET CAMPAIGNS AND A CONSERVATIVE COURT (PRE-1977)

The history of Ohio's judicial elections prior to the 1960s has not been well documented. The information that we have indicates that under the partisan election system that Ohio used until 1912, the two parties usually contested elections to the supreme court, and incumbents frequently suffered defeats (K. Hall 1984, 355, 363). After the adoption of the nonpartisan ballot for judicial elections, supreme court contests evoked lower levels of voter participation (K. Hall, 357–361), and there is some evidence that name recognition became increasingly important to electoral success (Aumann 1931, 414).

It appears that supreme court elections under the nonpartisan ballot generally were sleepy, below-the-radar contests, similar to most other judicial elections at the time. As late as the early 1970s, supreme court races were widely regarded as fairly unimportant, and elections were often decided by name recognition, more than a candidate's qualifications, policy preferences, or approach to the law (Barber 1972). Though Ohio was a highly competitive two-party state, especially during the 1960s, Republican supreme court candidates were usually successful at the polls (Barber 1971).[7]

As for the court's policies, Barber (1982, 40) writes that "the reputation of the Ohio Supreme Court is one of traditional deference to legislative policy-making and to established precedent." According to Tarr and Porter (1988, 127), "the Ohio high court was dominated from the close of the Civil War to 1978 by conservative, 'old stock' Republicans who fashioned the law to conform to the values and interests they shared with small town and rural Ohioans, with business and industry." As we discussed at the beginning of chapter 1, the court's actual record in tort policy in the twentieth century was not as conservative as those descriptions suggest. Still, the general perception was that not much was at stake in supreme court elections.

As a result, this era saw limited interest group involvement. That which did occur was generally behind the scenes in the form of small contributions or mobilization efforts among group members (e.g., union members). There were not massive efforts at widespread mobilization in support of or opposition to certain candidates. This quiescence was reflected in the levels of spending by candidates in the 1974–80 period, even as supreme court contests began to become more heated. The mean level of a candidate's spending was equivalent to about $100,000 in 2014 dollars, and no candidate spent as much as $300,000 in 2014 dollars (Barber 1982, 35).

THE PRO-PLAINTIFF CELEBREZZE COURT (1976–1986)

The focus on supreme court races began to change in the mid-1970s. Organized labor had long participated in supreme court contests at least to the extent of endorsing candidates. In 1976 the AFL-CIO increased its involvement in supreme court races in the form of publicity and funding for the two Democratic candidates, Ralph Locher and A. William Sweeney (Van Tine et al. 1998, 138). Both candidates were elected, winning two Republican-held seats that were vacated because of retirement, and the Democratic Party gained a majority on the court. Labor support did not necessarily give Locher and Sweeney their victories (Tarr and Porter 1988, 170–71), but those victories encouraged leaders of the Ohio labor movement to take a more active role in two 1978 races (Van Tine et al. 1998, 138–39).

Still, supreme court elections during this era were slow to take on the characteristics of new-style judicial campaigns discussed in the introduction. At the beginning of this era, interest groups remained primarily behind the scenes focusing on traditional tactics, such as mobilizing group members. By the end of the era, however, interest groups became full-fledged, highly visible participants in supreme court contests.

The 1978 elections are a good example of the delay in the inception of new-style campaigns. Democrats had just taken control of the court and Republicans had the opportunity to win back the majority if they could hold on to an open seat and beat incumbent Democrat William Brown. Additionally, the death of Chief Justice C. William O'Neill created what should have been a high-profile race for chief justice between two sitting justices, Democrat Frank Celebrezze and Republican Thomas Herbert.

But even with the growing involvement of the labor movement, the supreme court contests remained small in scale by current standards. As one newspaper article about the competitive race for chief justice noted, "neither candidate has the funds for a major media effort to draw attention to the race, nor will the contest generate much attention in terms of news stories" (Kermisch 1978). The articles that did exist regarding the three contests that year focused more on the horse race as opposed to substantive issues and a change in the direction of the court. Analysts believed that Celebrezze would benefit from the fact that his cousin, Anthony, was also on the ballot running for secretary of state. There was a fascination in the media coverage with the strange occurrence that three of the six candidates running for the high court had the last name Brown. Little information existed regarding the role of outside groups in the race other than generic statements about labor support of the Democratic candidates.

The lack of more extensive group involvement could be attributed to several factors. First, as we documented in chapter 1, the major shift in tort doctrine was not yet underway at the court. Because Democrat

Locher did not turn out to be a reliable vote for plaintiffs, the big policy changes did not come until the replacement of Republican justices by Clifford Brown in 1981 and James Celebrezze in 1983. Second, to win a court majority in 1978, business would have had to beat a popular incumbent in William Brown.[8] Third, because neither candidate for chief justice had to give up his seat, the majority of the court was not at stake as an outcome of this race. As a result, despite a tight race for a high-profile office, the election was not nearly as important as other races to come.

The elections two years later were much the same. Having ascended to chief justice in 1978 because of the death of the previous chief justice, Frank Celebrezze had to run for a full term in 1980. Again, interest group participation was minimal and media coverage was scarce. "At this point in the campaign," wrote one journalist in mid-October, "the Supreme Court candidates haven't done much that's obvious to the media or the voters" (St. Clair 1980). The United Automobile Workers' political action committee did support all three Democratic candidates, giving $10,000 to Celebrezze and $5,000 each to the other two Democratic candidates, while the Ohio State Medical Association PAC gave $2,000 to two of the Republican candidates running. These amounts are paltry in comparison to what was to come. And the races were dominated more by politics than by issues of concern to particular industries. Both parties were actively involved because of the controversial 4-3 decision along party lines to remove a Republican-backed redistricting initiative from the ballot.[9] Other issues included whether cameras should be allowed in the courtroom and upcoming cases regarding the death penalty and public funding for abortions. Although a one-vote swing on the court would have given the Republicans a majority, Celebrezze was never considered vulnerable as he was running against an underfunded Republican candidate.

Surprisingly, the race between incumbent Democratic justice Clifford Brown and Republican candidate David Dowd was extremely close with Brown winning only 50.6 percent of the vote. Yet the race was rarely discussed in the news media, and interest groups were not actively engaged even with the possibility of flipping the court. The lack of group involvement may have stemmed from the fact that interest groups had yet to fully realize the impact that they could have on policy by changing the makeup of the court. It just as easily could have been the case that, because of his well-known last name, Brown was not thought to be vulnerable.

After fairly quiet elections in 1982, in which Frank Celebrezze's brother,

James, defeated incumbent Blanche Krupansky and the Democrats obtained a 6-1 majority on the court, elections in 1984 and 1986 began to take on the characteristics of the new-style judicial campaigns.[10] According to Tarr and Porter (1988, 171), the 1984 elections "were unlike those previously experienced in Ohio. Media coverage was extensive, editorial support lopsidedly favored the Republican candidates and . . . undoubtedly had considerable effect on the electoral outcomes." The amount of money entering the 1984 supreme court races was unlike anything the state had seen before in a judicial race. Republican Craig Wright set a state record for spending by a supreme court candidate (roughly $375,000). James Celebrezze spent only about $175,000, but the state Democratic Party independently expended roughly $340,000 to defend the two Democratic-held seats (St. Clair 1985).

In light of the theoretical discussion of interest group involvement presented earlier, it is not a surprise that groups were considerably more active in these elections. Even with the inability of Republicans to win back the majority, the conditions were ripe for outside involvement. As we noted in chapter 1, by this time the court had moved in a clearly pro-plaintiff direction, and business groups were quite frustrated with the Celebrezze court. Although a swing seat was not at stake in 1984, the business community saw an opportunity to increase the number of Republicans on the bench because of the electoral vulnerability of James Celebrezze and an open seat to replace Democrat William Brown. Success in 1984 would set the stage for a takeover of the court in the 1986 elections. As a result, business groups became active participants in the 1984 elections.

What made the elections of 1984 and 1986 somewhat different from some large-scale supreme court elections in the state that came later was that the battles were primarily over politics and personality, not substance. The court was clearly moving to the left under Celebrezze's leadership, and groups such as trial lawyers, labor, business, and insurance were involved. But the elections in 1984 and 1986 appeared, in the media anyway, to be more of a referendum on Celebrezze's leadership and less about the direction that the court had moved on issues related to tort reform.

James Celebrezze's battle for reelection is a good example of the controversy surrounding his brother's leadership. The younger Celebrezze was caught in the crossfire between his brother and the state bar association. Frank Celebrezze had stripped the association of its authority to investigate ethics complaints against lawyers. (Some speculated that this was because the association rated James as unqualified.) The chief justice had a reputation for retribution when a person or group went against him. This was noted in an ad run by James Celebrezze's opponent Craig Wright, which quoted several newspaper articles critical of the court and said there was "danger in excess use of political power, especially when it is exercised for partisan political purposes."[11] The Republican Party also ran ads critical of the administrative policies of the Celebrezze court.

Another major issue in the race was the court's ruling that gave customers of Columbus and Southern Ohio Electric Company a reimbursement for being forced to pay for the Zimmer nuclear power plant.[12] Republicans viewed the decision as a political move by the Celebrezzes, since voters received reimbursement checks that included both brothers' names immediately before the election. However, many of the checks were for only a few cents, and the decision was roundly criticized in the media and by business groups that were upset with what they perceived to be an antibusiness tenor on the Celebrezze court. In fact, Frank Celebrezze blamed the utility refunds for the defeats of his brother and the other Democratic supreme court candidate (John Corrigan) running that year.[13]

The results of the 1984 races set the stage for an intense battle in 1986 for control of the court. A perfect storm regarding the conditions for interest group involvement took place. The court had clearly moved in a direction that was unpopular in the business community. As described in chapter 1, the court had handed down several recent controversial decisions related to torts and more important cases were on the horizon. There was a chance to flip the court, because after the results of the 1984 elections Democrats now held only a 4-3 majority and Chief Justice Celebrezze was up for reelection. Though Celebrezze was leading in early polls, the controversy surrounding his time as chief justice made him vulnerable. Given Celebrezze's record of supporting populist causes, business groups were willing to put substantial resources toward his ouster. Celebrezze did not shy away from confronting business and making his views on the direction of his court clear. After the 1984 defeats, he said that the court would continue to be "consumer oriented" and that changes were needed in the law of product liability and damages for emotional injuries.[14] Statements of this sort did not sit well with the business community.

The 1986 election for chief justice between Frank Celebrezze and Thomas Moyer is one of the most studied supreme court races in history. As figure 2.1 shows, with the exception of a 2000 contest, the race had more media coverage than any other race in Ohio from 1986 through 2012; it dwarfed the other two supreme court races on the ballot that year in coverage. The race was also the most expensive supreme court race in the state up to that point, and political parties and interest groups were extremely active, significantly more so than in previous elections. Business groups overwhelmingly backed Moyer, while labor remained the primary financier of Celebrezze's campaign, contributing more than $150,000 (Lowe and Treyens 1986).[15]

It is uncommon today, and was especially so during the 1980s, for a supreme court candidate's personality to be the center of the campaign. However, once again Celebrezze was the focal point. The Celebrezze court drifted to the left on issues like medical malpractice and workers' rights, and the chief justice was not shy about saying so. However, those issues were tertiary to the campaign. It was Celebrezze's personality, demeanor, and handling of the business of the court that were front and center, at least in the media. Republicans and Republican-backed groups argued that Celebrezze had politicized the chief justice position and complained that conflicts among the justices were now played out in public. Allegations that Celebrezze had mafia ties also were made, and he faced criticisms for tax issues related to an earlier campaign and for the use of a state airplane for travel to give political speeches.

This is not to say that substantive issues related to court rulings were absent from the race (Leonard 1989, 938–39). A few recent court rulings related to workers' compensation—especially two that allowed workers to sue if they were hurt on the job because an employer intentionally put them in a dangerous situation—nudged groups on both sides of the issue to be active. The Ohio Chamber of Commerce, the Ohio Manufacturers' Association, insurance groups, and farmers were particularly upset over the workers' compensation rulings. The business community's perception of Celebrezze was highlighted by an April 1986 article in *Forbes* magazine that included him in its list of "the hanging judges of business" (Greene 1986). Moyer made Celebrezze's support for labor a centerpiece of his campaign ads, including one in which he accused Celebrezze of accepting money from unions with ties to organized crime.

Republican supreme court candidates who were not facing Celebrezze also ran against him. Joyce George, who was matched against Democrat Herbert Brown, noted Celebrezze's ties to labor, stating that "when a leader of the court takes sides, that's not justice. That's injustice" (Yost 1986). George and incumbent Republican Robert Holmes ran a campaign advertisement against Celebrezze that showed an image of a collapsing scale of justice. While the scale of justice crumbles, a voiceover intones, "the Celebrezze court is the problem, and just voting out Frank Celebrezze isn't enough. Make sure Celebrezze can't control other supreme court justices. Restore balance with Justice Holmes and Judge George" (Curtin 1986).

On the other side, labor once again strongly supported Celebrezze, with one newspaper article saying that his political future was their "biggest concern" (St. Clair 1986). The United Steelworkers, for example, were forthright in their support for Celebrezze and his court's record: "The Ohio Supreme Court should remain a progressive, people's court—a court that has ruled in the favor of consumers on issues such a utilities, insurance and workers' compensation" (Lowe 1986). Although prohibited from making direct appeals for campaign contributions, Celebrezze regularly spoke before labor groups, highlighting the court's support for labor issues and noting the importance of labor's backing in maintaining a Democratic majority. Celebrezze continually criticized Moyer's campaign for being financed by business.

Even with strong financial support from labor unions, Celebrezze was unable to hold off Moyer, giving Republicans a majority once again for the first time since 1976. After his defeat, over the objections of several justices, Celebrezze continued to politicize the court by making sure that several cases of interest to his donors (dealing with workers' compensation, insurance, and utility law) were heard before he left the bench.

Ultimately, the Celebrezze-Moyer campaign was the least competitive of the three Ohio Supreme Court races that year. In fact, the two other contests between incumbent Republican Holmes and Democrat Francis Sweeney and an open-seat race between Republican George and Democrat Herbert Brown were each decided by less than 1 percent; Moyer won roughly 54 percent of the vote in his race. This is particularly interesting given the overwhelming amount of attention the race received, especially in comparison to the other contests that year (see figure 2.1). Had Democrats been able to defeat Holmes, for example, they could have retained a majority even with Celebrezze's loss. Or had Republicans been able to defeat Brown in the open seat, they would have held a majority of the seats on the court (assuming Holmes won) regardless of the outcome of the Celebrezze-Moyer contest. The candidates in these races complained frequently that they were being overshadowed by the Celebrezze-Moyer race, even though, as mentioned, Holmes and George made Celebrezze an issue in their campaigns.

This does not mean that interest groups ignored these two races. Indeed, the levels of spending in those races were quite high by historical standards—higher than in any contest in the 1980–84 period except for the James Celebrezze–Wright contest in 1984 (and probably higher than any of the contests of earlier decades). That interest groups did not focus even more on the associate justice contests reflected the fascination with Frank Celebrezze and the controversy over him. Nor was it obvious that the associate justice contests would be close, especially with Justice Holmes running as an incumbent.

CONTESTED CONTROL OF THE COURT (1987–1999)

The defeat of Frank Celebrezze in 1986 had potentially huge ramifications for the court. Republicans had control of the court for the first time since 1976.[16] However, the majority was slim (4-3), and gradually it became clear that Justice Andrew Douglas stood primarily on the pro-plaintiff side on tort issues. In 1992 the Republican advantage grew to 5-2. But the Republican who joined the court in that year, Paul Pfeifer, joined the pro-plaintiff side. Thus both sides had a strong incentive to battle for control of the court from the late 1980s through the 1990s.

In reality, there was considerable variation in the level of interest group involvement in supreme court contests during that period and corresponding variation in the scale of campaigns and media coverage of them. And on the whole, the level of campaign activity did not match what we might expect in light of the stakes that groups on both sides had in controlling the court. As figures 2.1 and 2.2 illustrate, media coverage and campaign contributions were minimal in several election years during this period (e.g., 1994 and 1998). Contentious issues that might spark involvement among pro-business or pro-plaintiff groups were present, but they were in the background, not the primary focus of the elections. And business and pro-plaintiff groups certainly contributed to candidates, but they were not central to the races. As one example, in Chief Justice Moyer's first reelection campaign in 1992, he was attacked by his Democratic opponent, Robert Gorman, more for not fixing the atmosphere of the court than for his pro-business rulings.[17] The lack of larger and more contentious supreme court contests in this period reflected both the determinants of interest group activity that we have described and some additional factors.

The 1988 elections for two seats on the court were similar in some respects to the contests for associate justice in 1986. In 1988, two Democratic seats were up for election. By historical standards the levels of spending by the candidates were high—overall, somewhat higher than in the associate justice races two years earlier. Interest groups were certainly involved in the 1988 contests. In fact, the Ohio AFL-CIO made it their highest election priority to hold on to the two Democratic-held seats on the court (see Curtin 1988). Labor unions were the largest contributors to Alice Robie Resnick's campaign, and the AFL-CIO and the United Auto Workers contributed more than $100,000 to the Ohio Democratic Party, which used the money for joint ads to support Resnick and incumbent Democratic justice A. William Sweeney (Lowe 1989). Democratic candidates also ran ads touting their endorsement by several labor unions.

But the investment and involvement by labor unions (or, on the other side, business) were not the same as in some of the more high-profile races, either previously or to come. The four candidates spent only a little more than $1 million across the full election year, compared with the roughly $2.8 million that Celebrezze and Moyer alone spent in 1986.[18] Roger Lowe (1988), reporting for the *Columbus Dispatch,* summarized the situation well: "The Supreme Court candidates spent record amounts in the 1986 elections, and many politicians—including the candidates themselves—expected the high costs of campaigning to spiral this year. But those high expectations have been chopped by reality to much lower levels, since campaign costs and public interest seem to be declining, not escalating."

Nor were the two contests very exciting. They revolved around judicial experience, background, and trying to tie Sweeney, in particular, to the problems with the Celebrezze court. In fact, the candidates, especially Resnick, complained that judicial canons prevented them from saying much of anything on the campaign trail.

In part, the lack of high-profile races in 1988 reflected perceptions of the stakes in the two contests. Republicans held a 4-3 majority, and with two Democratic seats up for reelection, partisan control of the court was not in play. Moreover, the liberalism of Republican justice Douglas on tort issues may not have been recognized to the extent that it was even two years later. Even so, business could have tried to increase its influence on a court that was closely divided ideologically, and pro-plaintiff groups preferred that the contested seats remain Democratic. Given that one of the two seats was to replace an incumbent who faced mandatory retirement, it would not have been surprising to see interest group involvement comparable to two years prior. Perhaps the key factor was the absence of former chief justice Frank Celebrezze, whose identity as a polarizing figure inspired involvement and interest in his 1986 contest that could not be matched in other contests.

It appeared that 1990 had the makings of an incredibly contentious, hotly contested election year. Republicans still held a slim 4-3 majority, but unlike two years earlier when both seats up for election were held by Democrats, the two seats contested in 1990 were occupied by Republicans. In other words, the majority of the court was up for grabs. Furthermore, in the previous year the court had voted to rehear several cases important to labor. Among them was a controversial 4-3 decision handed down right before the 1988 elections that a state law requiring binding arbitration in police and firefighter labor impasses—a law that labor groups favored—was unconstitutional as it applied to certain cities. When it reheard the case, the newly pro-labor court reversed the 1988 ruling.[19]

Yet, as illustrated by the limited media coverage of the races (see figure 2.1), the intense battle for the court one might have expected did not come to fruition. In fact, what is so remarkable about the 1990 supreme court elections is the lack of engagement by the Democratic Party and labor. By the end of 1989, Democrats did not have any clear candidates to challenge the sitting Republican justices (and did not appear to be in any hurry to recruit them).

A closer inspection of the races explains the relative silence of the Democratic Party and, more importantly for our purposes, of pro-plaintiff groups. The Democratic Party faced an uphill battle, even though a one-seat swing would have given it a majority on the court. The two Republican justices running for reelection were not vulnerable electorally. Justice Wright, who had defeated James Celebrezze in 1984 to earn his seat on the bench, was considered to be safe largely because of problems facing his Democratic opponents. The Democrats' first candidate, Mary Cacioppo, had to drop out of the race because of health concerns. Her replacement, Stephanie Tubbs Jones, struggled to gain traction because her husband and bailiff both had criminal records. Moreover, Wright criticized Jones mercilessly for what he said was her inability to keep up with her caseload. As a result, pro-plaintiff groups may have seen the attempt to beat Wright as an uphill battle and remained on the sidelines. Given Wright's electoral security, business groups likely also did not see the need to play an active role in the campaign. In hindsight, the calculation by pro-plaintiff groups to play a limited role in Jones's campaign may have been a mistake, as Wright only narrowly defeated her.

There was likely another reason for the lack of fireworks in the 1990 races. Justice Douglas, also up for reelection, was not a typical Republican. Although he was a traditional conservative on issues like crime, he was a strong supporter of labor. In fact, the state's AFL-CIO endorsed Douglas in the race because of his record on labor. He voted regularly to uphold the state's collective bargaining law for public employees and wrote the majority opinion overturning the controversial decision on binding arbitration. As a result of Douglas's pro-labor leanings, the Democratic Party was in a bind because it could not win labor's support of its candidate. On the other hand, business groups, who believed Douglas's record to be quite weak, found it difficult to challenge the Republican Party's candidate. As a result, they stayed out of the race as well.

As we have noted, the presence of Justices Douglas and Pfeifer (first elected to the bench in 1992) created an interesting dynamic on the court throughout the nineties. Although both justices were Republicans, they were strong supporters of labor and tort plaintiffs. As the *Columbus Dispatch* noted before Pfeifer's election, "On many issues, especially consumer and labor-business cases, the justices split into three factions. Moyer, Holmes, and . . . Wright have made up one faction, while two Democrats—Justices A. William Sweeney and Alice Robie Resnick—made up the other. [Justice Herbert] Brown and Douglas provided the swing votes on many decisions" (Ruth 1992).

Herbert Brown's decision not to run for reelection in 1992 surprised many and was thought to be a negative for labor. "From labor's point of view, we hate to see this happen," said John Hodges, Ohio AFL-CIO president, immediately after Brown announced he would not seek reelection. "We looked forward to working with him to be reelected. He hasn't always voted as we would hope, but overall he has been a good justice" (Yost 1991a).

However, the addition of Pfeifer, a former trial lawyer, to the bench ended up working in labor's favor. Although Republicans held a 5-2 majority on the court throughout much of the nineties, because of the support of Douglas and Pfeifer, there was essentially a 4-3 pro-plaintiff majority. Both justices were rated as among the least favorable to business interests on the court (see, e.g., Bradshaw 1996a). The presence of Douglas and Pfeifer on the bench also created strange campaign dynamics, because neither was embraced by their party elite or groups who backed their party. Both continued to be nominated by the GOP, yet it was labor that supported the candidates. Pfeifer's reelection in 1998 was particularly interesting. Douglas had been easily reelected two years before, receiving endorsements and support from both labor unions and trial lawyers. Business groups, including the insurance industry, had essentially remained on the sidelines because neither Douglas nor the Democratic candidate (Peter Sikora) were strong advocates for their concerns. In fact, as figure 2.2 indicates, few races saw fewer contributions to candidates than the Douglas-Sikora contest.

In 1998, business groups, including the Ohio Chamber of Commerce and the Ohio chapter of the National Federation of Independent Business, took a different tack and endorsed Pfeifer's opponent, Democrat Ronald Suster, even though Suster was given a "not recommended" rating by the Ohio State Bar Association. A nonprofit organization comprised primarily of business groups, Ohio Citizens Against Lawsuit Abuse, criticized Pfeifer because of his record expanding damage awards for successful plaintiffs and for his backing from trial lawyers. Conservatives were also incensed by Pfeifer's vote in a case that declared Ohio's school funding system to be unconstitutional. The court, in a 4-3 decision with Pfeifer considered to be the swing vote, ruled that the school funding plan was too reliant on property taxes, which led to disparities among school districts.[20] The ruling was attacked as judicial activism run amok. The ruling was not a high priority for business groups, but it did provide a potential issue to use against Pfeifer.

Opposition to Pfeifer by business was countered with support from pro-plaintiff groups. According to one report, Pfeifer received more than $400,000 from trial lawyers and lobbyists.[21] He easily defeated Suster, carrying roughly 70 percent of the vote. Again, Pfeifer's lack of electoral vulnerability and the strange tactic of business groups being forced to side with the Democratic candidate likely prevented more involvement from outside groups in this race.

Although many of the elections during this time period were fairly quiet affairs, a few races had higher profiles. In particular, the 1996 election between Republican Evelyn Stratton and Democrat Marianna Brown Bettman was a classic battle between business and trial lawyers. The race also saw a significant amount of outside spending, perhaps owing to a candidate spending cap put in place by the Ohio Supreme Court for the first time in that election cycle.[22] According to one report, "a coalition of unions and lawyers who represent plaintiffs in personal injury suits spent $234,000 backing Bettman and a group of interests that defend against such suits spent $170,500 backing Stratton" (Bradshaw 1996b). Because of the spending cap for candidates and the substantial independent activity by interest groups, the level of contributions shown in figure 2.2 does not fully portray the scale of campaign activity.

The reasons for outside groups' involvement in the Bettman-Stratton race went beyond limitations on candidate spending. This race was essentially an open seat; Justice Wright, a longtime supporter of business organizations, retired early to allow Stratton to be appointed to the bench by Republican governor George Voinovich. As a result, Stratton, although an incumbent, was not in as strong a position as she would have been had she previously won an election. Additionally, this race was particularly important because of an impending decision on a statute that limited damages for intangibles, such as pain and suffering. So, the conditions encouraged interest group involvement. Because of the unusual dynamics in the Douglas-Sikora race mentioned earlier and the fact that Douglas was considered to be safe, outside groups put their efforts and money into the Bettman-Stratton race. At the end of the day, Stratton won in a fairly convincing fashion, perhaps helped by the fact that the state Republican Party spent more than $300,000 supporting her campaign while the state Democratic Party spent only a few thousand in support of Bettman (Bradshaw 1996b).

In sum, the period between 1987 and 1999 saw some clashes between business groups on the one side and labor and trial lawyers on the other. Yet even with the partisan and ideological majorities of the court at stake throughout much of the time period, campaigns did not hit the fever pitch of those in 1984 and 1986. Some of this had to do with a concern immediately after Frank Celebrezze's defeat in 1986 about the increasingly political and contentious nature of the court. Some had to do with the fact that two Republicans who sat on the court during this time were supported by labor and trial lawyers because of their votes supporting those interests in tort cases. Business groups became increasingly frustrated with the rulings of the court on malpractice cases, and conservative groups were unhappy with the court's school funding decisions. However, because of Douglas and Pfeifer, their hands were often tied. That changed with the elections in 2000 and 2002.

BUSINESS FIGHTS FOR CONTROL OF THE COURT, AND WINS IN ITS SECOND TRY (2000–2002)

The 2000 judicial races were poised to be high-profile, contentious affairs. As the *Columbus Dispatch* wrote more than a year before the election, "both parties, along with business and labor groups, are gearing up for an all-out war in 2000" (Hallett 1999b). Although Chief Justice Moyer had made eliminating political contentiousness a focus, by the end of the decade the court was grappling with highly controversial cases that deeply divided the justices. The rulings in two cases in particular drew the ire of the business community. First, the decision that Ohio's method of funding public schools was unconstitutional was reaffirmed by the court, which gave the legislature a year to create an acceptable funding model.[23] Second, the court struck down a law passed by the Republican-controlled legislature and signed by a Republican governor limiting Ohioans' ability to sue for personal injury.[24] In both cases, the rulings were 4-3 and the majority opinion was written by Justice Resnick, who happened to be up for reelection in 2000.

Resnick was not the only justice up for reelection in 2000—Republican Deborah Cook was too—but it was Resnick's race that drew most of the attention from interest groups on both sides. The attention Resnick received was understandable, as the race had all of the characteristics that lead interest groups to become engaged in an election. Although Republicans had a 5-2 majority, in tort cases the court often divided along 4-3 lines, with Resnick in the majority along with Democrat Francis Sweeney and Republicans Douglas and Pfeifer. If the tort reform community could defeat Resnick, many of the laws capping damages that the court had declared unconstitutional could be reinstated. The court had continually frustrated the business and insurance communities by ruling against their interests. "Republicans control the court 5-2, and we lose decisions 4-3," said Mike Dawson, the press secretary for then senator George Voinovich, the person responsible for signing most of the tort bills into laws as governor (Hallett 1999a). As the *Columbus Dispatch* noted, "the current seven-member tribunal has gained a reputation as a 'plaintiff's court'" (ibid.). As a result, recent rulings certainly would have encouraged interest group involvement. Because several more important tort-related cases were likely to come before the court, the stakes were even higher. And last, although Resnick was an incumbent who had been elected six years earlier with 59 percent of the vote, the fact that she had written the majority opinion in several controversial cases made her a target.

The other supreme court race on the ballot in 2000, between incumbent Republican Cook and Democratic challenger Tim Black, did not get the same attention, although, as figures 2.1 and 2.3 indicate, it still was one of the more heavily covered races in our dataset and the candidates were frequently on the air.[25] Most likely the reason its visibility paled in comparison to the Resnick race is that Cook was part of the three-justice minority in the most controversial tort cases. Certainly pro-labor groups could have put their resources toward defeating Cook in case Resnick lost. Such an outcome would have preserved their 4-3 majority. However, Cook had won nearly 70 percent of the vote in 1994 and was considered safe. As a result, labor groups spent most of their time and resources defending Resnick.

Resnick's opponent was Republican Terrence O'Donnell, and the race had all the characteristics of a new-style judicial campaign. Substantial money was raised by candidates and spent by outside interest groups. Media coverage was frequent (in fact no contest in our dataset received more coverage; see figure 2.1), and the candidates, parties, and outside groups bombarded voters with campaign commercials, many of which were nasty (much to the chagrin of the candidates). Candidates, parties, and interest groups combined to air nearly 10,000 campaign ads, more than twice as many as in any other supreme court election in any state that year, and more than in any other election in our dataset (see figure 2.3). Interest groups were responsible for roughly half of the airings (Goldberg et al. 2002). In many ways, the campaign between Resnick and O'Donnell was more contentious than the infamous 1986 race between Frank Celebrezze and Thomas Moyer.

The amount of money spent independently by groups supporting both candidates was unprecedented in an Ohio Supreme Court race. As in 1996, this independent spending was partly the result of caps on spending by the candidates, all of whom had agreed to abide by the $550,000 spending limit in the general election period that was being challenged in court; ultimately, none of the candidates went far over that limit (Theis and Brown 2000).[26] Still, the amount of independent spending was stunning. Perhaps just as stunning was the number of groups putting money into the race, several of which were actually from out of state. Not surprisingly, the typical groups lined up to support Resnick (trial lawyers, unions) and O'Donnell (insurance and other businesses). Business was particularly active. A group called Citizens for a Strong Ohio, organized by the Ohio Chamber of Commerce, spent an estimated $5 million targeting Resnick for her support of trial lawyers.[27] The group was also supported by Republican governor Bob Taft, who played an active role in trying to defeat Resnick.

Citizens for a Strong Ohio received national attention for the harsh campaign ads it ran against Resnick. Most controversial was the ad in which Lady Justice is lifting her blindfold to peer at a pile of money. The announcer notes that the Resnick campaign had received $750,000 from trial lawyers since 1994 and voted with the group's interest 70 percent of the time. The ad closes by asking the question, "Is justice for sale in Ohio?" It was roundly criticized by government watchdog groups, and it triggered a complaint to the Ohio Election Commission over the truthfulness of the ad.[28] Additionally, the Institute for Legal Reform, another organization backed by the Ohio Chamber of Commerce, spent roughly $1 million on campaign advertising with essentially the same message.

Citizens for a Strong Ohio also raised concerns about the influence of trial lawyers in a fund-raising letter to potential supporters. The letter, signed by the presidents and CEOs of Nationwide Insurance, Ormet Primary Aluminum, and AK Steel and the former president of Ashland Oil, stated that the "composition of the Supreme Court may be more important than the composition of the legislature." It closed with an admonition: "Remember this: By a slim 4-3 margin, the Ohio Supreme Court chronically does the bidding of our state's labor bosses and personal-injury attorneys. That's wrong, and we can change it by acting now!" (Johnson 2000).

While Citizens for a Strong Ohio received the most attention for its involvement in the race, it was hardly alone. In fact, the race was dominated by a plethora of groups all leveling the same charge against Resnick. Ohioans for Fair and Independent Judges, a PAC comprised of insurance companies and other businesses, primarily the Ohio Manufacturers' Association, supported O'Donnell, as did Ohio Citizens Against Lawsuit Abuse.

The groups condemning Resnick were not confined to Ohio. Americans for Job Security, a group based in Virginia, attacked Resnick via a radio spot almost a year before the election. The ad criticized Resnick's opinion in the case earlier that summer striking down a law limiting damages in product-liability lawsuits. It was the first time the group had targeted a supreme court candidate (Hallett 1999b). Another national group, Citizens for a Sound Economy, also attacked Resnick as being in the pockets of trial lawyers. And while the Ohio Chamber of Commerce was the primary organization opposed to Resnick, its counterpart up north actually got involved as well. The Michigan Chamber of Commerce sponsored newspaper ads encouraging Ohio businesses to move to Michigan because of an "activist Ohio Supreme Court" that has given "Michigan a tremendous edge over Ohio in the battle for jobs" (Hallett 2000a). The US Chamber of Commerce also ran several television commercials criticizing Resnick for her relationship with trial lawyers.

Trial lawyers and labor organizations were far from silent and actively defended Resnick. A group of trial attorneys and labor organizations, led by the Ohio Education Association because of Resnick's opinion in the school funding case, created Justice 2000, whose sole goal was to help Resnick defend her seat. The PAC hired the former chair of the Ohio

Democratic Party to serve as its head. Additionally, a group called Citizens for an Independent Court, composed of trial lawyers, unions, teachers, and people in law enforcement, spent more than $1.5 million independently in support of Resnick and Black (Hallett 2000b). And the Ohio Academy of Trial Lawyers spent roughly $1 million on behalf of Resnick (Bradshaw 2000).

Despite all the money spent by the candidates, parties, and independent groups, after Election Day the makeup of the court remained the same. Resnick beat O'Donnell, winning a solid 57 percent of the vote. In the undercard election, Republican justice Cook barely defeated the Democratic candidate Black, 52 percent to 48 percent.

The battle in 2000 set the stage for another set of nasty campaigns in 2002, especially after business interests failed to win the court majority. Because of the retirement of Justice Douglas, forced by the state's age limit, the 4-3 pro-labor and pro-tort plaintiff majority was threatened. Additionally, the school funding issue that the court had grappled with for years (and on which Douglas was in the 4-3 majority) was back on the docket. As a result, conditions were such that groups on both sides of the issue were poised to spend substantial money trying to influence the court.

Two seats were up for election in 2002. In the contest to replace Douglas, lieutenant governor Maureen O'Connor, a Republican, faced Tim Black, the Democratic candidate who had lost two years earlier in a close race against Justice Cook. The second race featured incumbent Republican justice Evelyn Stratton, a target of labor six years earlier during her first election, and Cuyahoga County Common Pleas Court judge Janet Burnside, a Democrat. As figures 2.1, 2.2, and 2.3 illustrate, these races stood out in terms of newspaper coverage, campaign contributions, and television advertisements. In fact, candidates in these races combined to raise more money (controlling for inflation) than in any other election year in the period between 1992 and 2012, including the 2000 contests.

Once again, these two races were battles between insurance and other business groups on the one side and labor and trial lawyers on the other. Five different independent groups spent substantial amounts of money in support of their preferred candidates. According to one report, outside groups spent roughly $6 million on television and radio commercials, and the four candidates combined to spend approximately $6.2 million, most of which came from the independent groups, making it the most expensive supreme court election cycle in the state's history (Craig 2003). Citizens for a Strong Ohio was active once more in this election cycle, although its leaders shied away from running controversial ads like "Is Justice for Sale in Ohio?" and this time they disclosed their contributors (primarily insurance companies and the Ohio Chamber of Commerce). In this election the organization stayed positive and produced radio ads promoting Stratton's background.

Instead, it was a new organization, Informed Citizens of Ohio, that caused controversy because of its efforts to politicize the Stratton-Burnside race. The group was led by the Republican Speaker of the Ohio House of Representatives and an Akron businessman who typically supported conservative causes.[29] In one ad sponsored by the group, viewers saw a vacated doctor's office while an announcer said, "Little by little doctors are disappearing from the state of Ohio. Disappearing because frivolous lawsuits are forcing them to leave their practices. And when it's your doctor, where do you go? Justice Evelyn Stratton's record shows that she understands the need to stop lawsuit abuse and now so do you."[30] Ohioans could not escape the races for the supreme court even when visiting actual doctors' offices. Some physicians who were concerned about rising medical malpractice premiums handed out literature supporting the Republican candidates.

Stratton drew criticism for mailing fund-raising letters signed by the state's Republican attorney general and governor calling Stratton the "most 'pro-business' justice on the Supreme Court." The Republican candidate for attorney general that year, who could expect to appear before Stratton in court were they both to win, also raised money on her behalf. Stratton attended a rally at the statehouse to support proposed medical malpractice insurance legislation (Craig 2002b).

Those on the left were not silent either. Citizens for an Independent Court ran the ad "Two Sides," which accused Stratton and O'Connor of putting "large corporations ahead of working families."[31] The ad was criticized by the Ohio State Bar Association.[32] Stratton's nickname, "the Velvet Hammer," was mentioned in two other ads by the group, although not in a positive way. "Eve Stratton calls herself the velvet hammer. Yeah, corporations get the velvet, Ohio families get the hammer. We need Justices who protect people, not corporations."[33]

In the Black-O'Connor contest, Black was an unabashed supporter of labor who drew criticism for stating in a speech that Douglas's seat was "labor's seat." Unlike many supreme court races in which the candidates themselves remain above the fray, Black went negative on O'Connor, accusing her of being a career politician and in the pockets of insurance companies and doctors. "The other side is pretty clear on how they intend to rule on tort reform and school funding," Black said, "and I think that's wrong" (Craig 2002a).

Since the O'Connor-Black contest was for an open seat to replace the pro-labor Republican Douglas, one might have expected it to receive even more attention than the Stratton-Burnside contest. But spending and media attention was roughly comparable between the two contests, with both at an unusually high level, and several commercials that ran on television focused solely on the Stratton-Burnside contest. The reason appears to be the expectation that even with Stratton's incumbency advantage, her contest would be closer. O'Connor had built up a strong lead over Black in the polls, perhaps because of name recognition generated from her time as the state's lieutenant governor and chairwoman of the Ohio Security Task Force, a body created by Governor Taft after the September 11 attacks.

In contrast, polling for the Stratton-Burnside race indicated that it was tight. At some point labor and trial lawyers appeared to concede the Douglas seat to O'Connor, hoping that they could defeat Stratton instead and maintain a slim 4-3 majority on the court that often ruled in favor of their interests. On the other hand, business and insurance groups, knowing that they were likely to pick up Douglas's seat, realized that they needed to defend Stratton. Otherwise, the court would essentially retain its status quo as it related to issues such as tort reform.

On Election Day, both O'Connor and Stratton had convincing victories. Their success likely owed something to each of the following: the popularity that year of Republican candidates, who swept all statewide races; O'Connor's and Stratton's visibility as statewide elected officials; and an effective campaign by the business community, tying the Democratic candidates to medical malpractice abuse and worrying voters about the quality of the health care that they would receive as a result.

As we documented in chapter 1, the reelection of Stratton and the replacement of pro-labor Douglas with pro-business O'Connor dramatically changed the direction of the court on tort-related issues. Almost immediately, the court began handing down pro-business decisions. As just two examples, the court ruled within a year of the 2002 elections that companies are not liable for insurance claims by employees injured or killed in non-work-related accidents and overturned a previous ruling that allowed relatives of an employee to file claims for accidents unrelated to the employee's job.[34] When the court made its initial 4-3 ruling in 1999 regarding the first issue, Justice Douglas wrote the opinion.[35] Justice O'Connor, his replacement on the bench, wrote the opinion overturning the initial decision.

A PRO-BUSINESS COURT (2003–PRESENT)

The replacement of Justice Douglas with Justice O'Connor gave business a majority of the court, and that advantage has only gotten stronger since then. In 2004 the majority grew to 5-2, with only one Democrat and maverick Republican Paul Pfeifer on the pro-plaintiff side. After the 2006 election the court was all Republican, a situation that lasted until Democrat William O'Neill won an unexpected victory in 2012. That victory was the only one for a Democratic candidate in the sixteen contested races between 2004 and 2016. Moreover, few contests have been close; six of the Republican victories were by more than a 60-40 margin. News coverage of recent elections has been relatively limited (see figure 2.1).

Although levels of spending by the candidates have remained high by historical standards, they seldom rival the most visible contests in earlier periods. The only exceptions were two contests for associate justice, between Judith Lanzinger and Nancy Fuerst in 2004 and between Yvette McGee Brown and Sharon Kennedy in 2012. By the 1990s, most Republican candidates were able to raise and spend more than their Democratic rivals, but that has been even more true in the elections from 2004 on. Virtually all GOP candidates have had a significant monetary advantage over their Democratic opponents.[36] Labor, so active in the 1990s and early 2000s, has essentially stayed on the sidelines since.

The limited help that Democratic candidates received from pro-plaintiff groups after 2004 is understandable. The sweep of the 2004 contests by Republican candidates and the resulting solidification of the court's pro-business majority undoubtedly discouraged groups on the other side from undertaking large-scale efforts to win seats on the court. That was especially true of the wide margin of defeat for Nancy Fuerst, whose spending level was about the same as that of each Democratic candidate in 2002.

But it is noteworthy that labor did not play a larger role in 2004. With Justice O'Connor's replacement of Justice Douglas, the court crafted several 4-3 decisions that labor opposed. Given what was at stake and the fact that four seats on the court were up for election in 2004, labor should have made a concerted effort to win back their 4-3 majority.[37] Two justices who were part of the 4-3 pro-business, tort reform majority were up for election (Moyer and O'Donnell). Labor was helped when Justice

Pfeifer, also up for election, did not face opposition in the Republican primary and was unopposed in the general election as well. Pfeifer's uncontested election meant that labor only had to defend the open seat created by Justice Francis Sweeney's retirement. In other words, if labor could have defeated either Moyer or O'Donnell and retained Sweeney's seat with a labor-friendly candidate, then they once again would have had a majority on the court.[38]

This scenario was not implausible. Given that O'Donnell was newly appointed and had not won election to the bench, he was likely to be vulnerable. According to one late August poll, all races were within the margin of error (Democratic candidates Nancy Fuerst and William O'Neill, O'Donnell's challenger, held statistically insignificant leads over their opponents while Chief Justice Moyer held only a two percentage-point margin over his opponent), and roughly three out of four voters were undecided in all three races (Rowland 2004). Yet, as the election progressed, voters essentially heard from only one side. Fuerst's own substantial spending was outpaced by her opponent Lanzinger, and in the other contests the Republican candidates had enormous spending advantages over their Democratic opponents.

The advantages of the Republicans in their own campaign spending were extended enormously by spending from independent groups, which paid an estimated $2 million for television time alone (Goldberg et al. 2005, 54). In mid-campaign, it was reported that about $10 million had been spent on the four races, about $9 million for the three Republicans running in contested races. More than half of this $9 million was donated or spent directly by the Ohio Chamber of Commerce, insurance companies, doctors, and hospitals (Craig 2004). Citizens for a Strong Ohio ran television and radio ads on behalf of O'Donnell and Lanzinger, and the group Ohio Patients for a Fair Court distributed writing tablets in the waiting rooms of doctors' offices supporting the two and Moyer.

No such efforts appeared to exist on the other side. Lawyers—mostly trial lawyers, it can be presumed—contributed about three-quarters of a million dollars to Fuerst. But contributions from labor unions to the three Democrats were more limited than in 2002, and no interest groups sponsored their own TV commercials for the Democratic candidates. It may be that the limited resources of a declining labor movement in Ohio did not allow for a massive commitment to the supreme court campaigns when there were other elections important to the movement—including a presidential contest in which Ohio played a critical role.

In the end, the Republicans easily won all three seats, giving them a

6-1 advantage on the court and giving business and insurance groups a 5-2 voting majority. O'Donnell cruised to an easy victory, carrying more than 60 percent of the vote. O'Donnell's victory may be explained at least in part by the fact that the Democratic candidate in the race was someone the party did not support in the primary and who essentially refused to spend money on his campaign. Had the Democrats fielded a stronger candidate, perhaps labor would have been more involved.[39] Despite having substantial funding for her campaign, Nancy Fuerst lost by a 57-43 margin. Ironically, the closest contest was for chief justice: the three-term incumbent Thomas Moyer won only 53 percent of the vote against C. Ellen Connally despite her lack of preexisting name recognition and her seriously underfunded campaign. With substantial support from pro-plaintiff groups, Connally might well have won.

Since 2004, pro-tort reform groups have continued their record of success in elections to the supreme court. In 2006, even with the Democratic Party sweeping almost all other statewide offices, Republicans won both seats for the court. Once again, the Republican candidates easily raised more money than the Democratic candidates, and labor was not especially active in either race.[40] Labor groups donated roughly $100,000 to Democratic candidate Ben Espy, but there was no evidence that they ran advertisements on his behalf. Nor did Espy's small number of campaign ads mention labor's support of him, not even a brief ad that specifically mentioned those endorsing Espy. Instead, the few advertisements in these races focused primarily on the traditional judicial election issues of experience and competence. Because Justice Resnick retired and was replaced by a Republican (Robert Cupp), Republicans had a 7-0 monopoly on the court. Justice Pfeifer was the only justice with pro-plaintiff leanings.

More recent elections have followed the same script. In 2008 there was little media coverage of either supreme court contest (see figure 2.1). Both Republican incumbents (O'Connor and Stratton) easily won and outspent their Democratic opponents substantially. Labor groups gave only roughly $75,000 combined to the two Democratic candidates. Once again, the Republican candidates were funded heavily by groups with business backgrounds, including the Ohio Chamber of Commerce. According to a consultant for the two Democratic candidates, a group affiliated with the chamber, Partnership for Ohio's Future, raised several thousand dollars from defendants in an asbestos case decided shortly before the election, in which O'Connor and Stratton were part of a 5-2 majority, making it more difficult to file asbestos-related lawsuits

(Nash 2008).[41] The low-profile nature of the 2008 races may have owed something to a competitive presidential election in the state that overshadowed the court contests. However, it is not likely that either race would have been hotly contested even without the presidential election. Neither O'Connor nor Stratton was vulnerable, and defeating both would not have changed the court majority on tort issues.

In 2010, Republican candidates again won easily. Pfeifer ran unopposed and remained the only consistently pro-plaintiff justice. Two other seats were at stake, one held by Justice Lanzinger and the other essentially an open seat for chief justice. Chief Justice Moyer died in April of that year. Democratic governor Ted Strickland made an interim appointment of Democrat Eric Brown, who immediately was up for election and was challenged by Justice O'Connor. Partnership for Ohio's Future once again ran commercials on behalf of both Republicans, touting, among other things, the duo's record of "help[ing] businesses compete and create more jobs."[42] Both Republican candidates easily outspent their Democratic opponents, who received most of their support from trial lawyers. No outside groups appeared to run advertisements on their behalf. With the two Republican victories, the Democratic Party had not won a seat on the court since Justice Resnick fended off a difficult challenge in 2000.

The 2012 elections can only be described as bizarre. Democrats maintained representation on the court because Strickland got to appoint O'Connor's replacement when she became chief justice. He chose Yvette McGee Brown, the state's first African American female justice, who had to run for election in the next general election. Particularly interesting was the fact that McGee Brown and O'Connor developed a friendship and the Republican chief justice pledged to stay out of the race. Some of the closeness may have been owing to McGee Brown's record on the bench in cases involving business. McGee Brown had served as the former head of the Center for Child and Family Advocacy at Nationwide Children's Hospital, where she had cultivated relationships with many business leaders. McGee Brown's background with the business community did not go unnoticed by former Ohio Republican Party chairman Robert Bennett. "Yvette has an understanding of business," said Bennett. "It makes her a very difficult opponent for Republicans" (Candisky 2012).

McGee Brown was able to raise more funds than her Republican opponent, Sharon Kennedy, the first time in several election cycles that a Democratic candidate did so. Brown's business background did not dissuade labor, who still contributed almost $100,000 to her campaign, while trial lawyers gave roughly $300,000.[43] Yet even with her solid war chest, McGee Brown appears to have run only one ad, which touted her ability to get along with her Republican colleagues. There is no record of the Democratic Party or other outside groups running ads on her behalf. On the other hand, Kennedy was frequently on the airwaves (either with her own commercials or commercials supported by the Republican Party) touting her background on crime. In the end, although McGee Brown outspent Kennedy, had the implicit backing of the Republican chief justice, and was recommended "highly" by the Ohio State Bar Association compared to Kennedy—who was rated "not qualified"—she lost the election, winning only 43 percent of the vote.

The race between McGee Brown and Kennedy was not the most surprising one for supreme court in 2012. That honor goes to the contest between incumbent Republican Robert Cupp and his Democratic opponent William O'Neill. O'Neill had run for the high court unsuccessfully twice before, was not endorsed by the Democratic Party in the primary, barely qualified for the ballot, and spent a total of just over $5,000 on his primary and general election campaigns. Yet he defeated Cupp, who raised close to $750,000 and became the first Republican supreme court candidate to lose in over a decade.

As he did in his earlier campaigns, O'Neill attacked his opponent for soliciting substantial sums of money from groups who appear before the court. The race became particularly nasty when an ad run by the Republican Party accused O'Neill of expressing sympathy for rapists.[44] Partnership for Ohio's Future also ran an ad in favor of Cupp, praising him for his old-fashioned values and integrity and noting that he had support from groups that included small business, law enforcement, and doctors.[45] With the losses by the two incumbents (McGee Brown and Cupp) and Justice O'Donnell's reelection, Republicans maintained a 6-1 majority on the bench. They maintained that advantage once again in 2014 when two Republican incumbents were easily reelected in races that received little coverage and had minimal campaign advertising. In 2016, Republicans swept all three seats up for election, including Chief Justice O'Connor's unopposed bid for reelection.

The dearth of competitive elections and the lopsided involvement of groups during this period can be explained by the increasing domination of business interests on the court. A snowball effect started in 2002. Following an impressive victory in 2000, labor suffered crushing defeats in 2002. The elections in 2004 should have had substantial outside involvement by both labor and business groups, given the recent pro-defendant shift in court policy and the fact that the court was still divided on the issue. Yet only one side showed up for the fight. Perhaps in part because of a weak set of Democratic candidates, labor stayed on the sidelines.

After Republican victories in 2004, two things happened. First, after dominating elections for the last several cycles, more Republicans sat on the bench and, given their incumbency status, were less likely to be vulnerable electorally. Second, because Republicans controlled the court there was no opportunity for labor to flip the court. As a result, business protected its interests on the court while labor seemed to turn its attention elsewhere.

Conclusion

This chapter analyzed the variation in campaign visibility and the involvement of interest groups in supreme court elections. There are trends evident in the history of Ohio Supreme Court elections. When certain groups' interests, especially those in insurance, the health industry, and other business sectors, are threatened by recent court rulings, they become active in judicial campaigns, donating substantial amounts of money to candidates and spending independently on the candidates' behalf. This involvement is heightened when there is the potential to swing the majority in the group's favor and when incumbents either are not running for reelection or are vulnerable electorally.

The story in Ohio is fairly straightforward. Threatened by the left-leaning Celebrezze court, business, insurance, and health groups worked to elect a majority that would support their positions on issues such as tort reform. Although Republicans won a majority in 1986 and maintained it in subsequent elections, the groups that traditionally supported Republican judicial candidates did not have control of the court because of two left-leaning Republicans who were supportive of tort plaintiffs. In both high-profile and lower-profile races, the business sector helped to elect friendly justices who were generally supportive of their concerns. Since that time, this faction has controlled the court and, as a result, more recent Ohio Supreme Court races have been largely quiet affairs.

To win control of the court, the business community tried several messages. Occasionally it attacked someone's moral compass, such as was the case in the Moyer-Celebrezze race. A candidate's experience or competence was also fair game. And sometimes the groups ran ads that specifically mentioned issues directly related to torts, such as medical malpractice. For the most part, however, business groups cast their issue-related messages in broad strokes, attacking "activist" judges and focusing on how the election of their preferred candidate would improve the business climate or health care. Concerns about torts were the driving force behind business involvement, but the public would not necessarily see it as such.

This chapter traced the involvement of these groups in the judicial campaigns. We have a sense of how successful they were because we know the outcomes of the races. What we do not know is whether or how their involvement influenced voters. We have discussed the first two stages of a cycle so far: the court moves in a direction that is not popular with a certain group (chapter 1) and that group mobilizes and becomes active in judicial campaigns (chapter 2). We need to complete the cycle by understanding how the campaigns by those groups influenced voters. We turn to that question in the next chapter.

THREE

Voters' Responses to Electoral Campaigns

The analyses in chapter 1 showed that the tort policies of the Ohio Supreme Court changed substantially over the period from the mid-1980s to the mid-2000s, with the court taking a pro-plaintiff position in some periods and a pro-defendant position in others. The key source of these policy changes was changes in the membership of the court. In turn, that membership change reflected the outcomes of contested elections to the court.

The most recent shift in the court's policies, coming after the 2002 elections, was in a pro-defendant direction. That shift was reinforced by the outcomes of the contests that followed in 2004 and 2006, and since then the court has had a solid pro-defendant majority. This result was a triumph for business groups that had mobilized as a result of their dissatisfaction with the court's liberal tort policies in the early 1980s.

The three questions that we address in this chapter concern the sources of that result. The first question is why a series of elections ultimately produced the pro-defendant court that the business community had sought. The second question is a subset of the first: how much did efforts by the business community contribute to that result? We give special emphasis to that second question because it involves one of the linkages among court policy, campaign efforts, and election outcomes that are at the heart of the book. The third question concerns voters' intentions: to what extent did they act deliberately to change court policy? We analyze the behavior of voters at the individual and collective levels to address those questions.

Because of our focus in chapter 2 on interest group activity, the answer to our first two questions might seem to merge: election outcomes ultimately produced the court that the business community sought because of the efforts of that community—contributing large amounts of money in contributions to its favored candidates and, beginning in the late 1990s, spending money on its own in support of those candidates. But some complications need to be taken into account. The triumph of pro-defendant groups came only after two decades of efforts. Election outcomes did not always favor the interests of business groups even when those groups made massive commitments to favored candidates. For one thing, pro-plaintiff groups made their own very substantial efforts to match the impact of business groups. And business groups faced the obstacle created by two Republican justices who took strong pro-plaintiff positions unexpectedly and who were effectively impossible to defeat once they were in office. That turn of events underlines the reality that the outcomes of supreme court contests are shaped by forces that are beyond the control of the contending groups on both sides.

Even with all these complications, we do find that spending by the business community had significant impact on election outcomes and thus on the court's membership. That finding raises important questions about voters' intent. Through their collective choices, Ohio's voters changed the tort policies of the supreme court and thereby gave the business community what it wanted. Did they do so consciously and deliberately, weighing the merits of tort policy and choosing to strengthen the position of defendants? Were they influenced by the campaigns that business groups supported, but for reasons that had nothing to do with the policy issues that were at stake? Or was their role partly conscious and partly unconscious? The validity of these competing possibilities is an important issue for our understanding of supreme court elections as mechanisms of public influence over judicial policy.

Our inquiry in this chapter relies primarily on two sources of information. The first is aggregate data on all supreme court contests between 1980 and 2014. By analyzing the relationship between attributes of those contests and the behavior of potential and actual voters, we can probe the determinants of election outcomes and the role of campaign activity in producing those outcomes.

The second source is a series of surveys that were conducted in Ohio between 1984 and 2006, surveys that included questions about vote choices in supreme court contests and potential determinants of those choices. The attributes of those surveys merit some discussion.

Units within the Department of Political Science at Ohio State University conducted surveys of Ohioans in all the gubernatorial election years from 1986 through 2006, as well as the presidential election years of 1984 and 1988. In every survey, respondents were asked about their participation and choices in the state supreme court contests in that year.[1] The surveys also contained questions concerning possible determinants of the vote and other aspects of political knowledge and attitudes.

In each of these election years, surveys were conducted shortly after the general election. Potential respondents were identified with the goal of achieving as close to a random sample of adult citizens as possible. Each survey was conducted by telephone.

This set of surveys has limitations for our purposes. One limitation is inherent to efforts to probe voting for offices below the top levels. Because voters do not focus on those contests, the bases for their votes—and even the votes themselves—may fade in their memories after the election.

Beyond this general limitation, there are some limitations specific to the Ohio surveys that we use. Most obviously, they were conducted in only a subset of election years, and one of the years without a survey (2000) featured the most dramatic battle between pro-plaintiff and pro-defendant groups. Questions asked of voters varied somewhat from year to year, and some other aspects of the survey design varied as well. Finally, the sets of questions that were related to supreme court elections did not focus on our concerns as much as we would like.

All this being true, the surveys nonetheless are a valuable resource for our purposes. There is no other long series of election surveys that include questions about supreme court elections (or elections to any other court) in any state. Thus, the Ohio series gives us a unique basis for analysis of voters' choices across election years and specific contests. Further, the questions that were included in the surveys do provide considerable information that is relevant to the issue of why voters responded to the supreme court campaigns as they did. If the election surveys that we use fall well short of the ideal, they also provide an extraordinary body of information to help us in probing voters' responses to contests for the Ohio Supreme Court.

We begin this chapter by considering in general terms how voters respond to supreme court contests and why they respond as they do. Our inquiry into influences on the Ohio court's elections then proceeds in several steps. In the second section we analyze the determinants of the shares of the vote won by pro-plaintiff and pro-business candidates. The third section shifts the level of analysis from vote shares to individual voters, probing the determinants of their decisions whether to cast votes in supreme court contests and their choices between candidates. The fourth section probes the extent to which voters deliberately acted to produce the set of election outcomes that ultimately brought about a court favorable to the business community. In the final section, we examine the evidence presented in the chapter to reach our best judgment about the sources of success for the business community.

Voters and Supreme Court Contests

We can think about voting behavior in any election in terms of information processing: campaigns and other sources communicate information that potential and actual voters use to make choices (see Sniderman, Brody, and Tetlock 1991, chap. 9; Zaller 1992, chap. 10). What we know about the impact of campaigns and other sources of information during the campaign period comes primarily from contests in which the volume of information available to voters is relatively high, especially presidential elections (e.g., Bartels 1993; Hillygus and Jackman 2003; see also Lodge, Steenbergen, and Brau 1995). Because the volume of information that is available to voters tends to fluctuate substantially across offices, voters respond to contests for those offices differently (Hinckley, Hofstetter, and Kessel 1974; Hinckley 1976; Shaffer 1982).

The key attribute of most contests for state supreme courts—and for that matter, most contests for the preponderance of other elected offices—is the dearth of information that voters assimilate. In part, this is because of the small volume of information that is available to them. To the extent that information *is* available, voters' learning of this information is limited by the lack of prominence of most supreme court contests. Where supreme court contests are conducted simultaneously with more visible contests, as they are in the great majority of states, information about the supreme court contests may be drowned out by information about the other contests. Further, voters usually have weaker incentives to learn about contests for judgeships than contests for offices that they see as more important.

One result of this situation is high roll-off. In the preponderance of elections that include contests for state supreme courts, few if any voters decide to go to the polls because they want to vote in those contests specifically; at least the great majority go because they care about other offices or simply because they want to participate in an election. Once voters are at the polls, it is common for them to skip supreme court contests (Dubois 1980, chap. 2; Hall and Bonneau 2008) and other judicial contests (Streb, Frederick, and LaFrance 2009; Shortell 2013). The phenomenon of skipping certain offices can be understood as the product of voters' sense that they have too little information to make a choice between candidates (Wattenberg, McAllister, and Salvanto 2000).

When voters do choose between judicial candidates, the small volume of information that they typically possess makes them heavily reliant on the information that is least costly, information that the ballot itself provides. Voters who have little information about candidates on the ballot may respond to those candidates on the basis of simple name recognition (Kam and Zechmeister 2013). That recognition may be mistaken, and the annals of judicial elections provide numerous examples of supreme court candidates who benefited from a name that had positive associations because of other people who held it.

The classic case occurred in Texas in 1976, when a candidate was elected to the supreme court on the basis of the resemblance between his name and that of two well-known politicians. The victorious candidate was already the subject of a disbarment effort. After his election he was recorded in a conversation indicating his interest in having two people killed, was indicted for aggravated perjury and forgery, was convicted on the perjury charge, resigned under pressure, and received a seven-year sentence for jumping bail after he failed to return to the United States to serve his sentence (Holder 1980; Kritzer 2015, 36–37). It is fair to say that in this instance voters' lack of information was costly.

If voters know something substantive about the candidate whose name they recognize or think they recognize, they can apply that knowledge to their choice. Thus, even voters who have paid no attention to the campaigns for a supreme court seat can act on information they gleaned prior to the campaign period.

Names also provide clues to candidates' ethnicity and gender. Voters might respond positively or negatively to those perceived attributes of candidates in themselves (Mueller 1970; Byrne and Pueschel 1974; Nakanishi, Cooper, and Kassarjian 1974), as they sometimes do in judicial elections (Dubois 1984; Klumpp 2011). They may also make inferences from those perceived attributes that help guide their choices, such as the guess that female and African American candidates are relatively liberal (McDermott 1997, 1998).[2]

Overall, the most powerful piece of information that the ballot can disclose is the candidates' political party affiliations. In an information-poor situation, voters who favor one party over the other—the great majority—can choose a candidate on the basis of that preference. Thus, partisan judicial elections tend to elicit high levels of party-line voting, much higher than those conducted with a nonpartisan ballot.[3] In the process, they reduce the impact of other information that can be inferred from the ballot (see Kam 2007).

In states with nonpartisan supreme court elections, voters may still be aware of candidates' party affiliations from sources other than the ballot. The parties sometimes publicize candidates' affiliations on sample ballots and in other forms. Candidates' names can provide clues to party affiliations, based on perceived ethnicity or the specific name. In Ohio, with its unique combination of partisan primaries and nonpartisan general elections to the supreme court, primary election campaigns and ballots may plant a candidate's party in voters' minds. But direct information about party affiliations is more costly to voters in nonpartisan states than in those that use a partisan ballot.

Information about candidates' actual or prospective performance as justices is considerably higher in cost. It is usually very difficult for voters to obtain direct information about the quality of an incumbent's work on the court or the substantive content of a justice's votes and opinions on an issue. It is even more difficult for them to gauge the likely quality or content of a nonincumbent's prospective work as a justice. A candidate's party affiliation provides a clue to ideological leanings, but the clue is imperfect. As we showed in chapter 1, a voter who inferred conservatism on tort issues from the Republican affiliations of Andrew Douglas and Paul Pfeifer would have gotten things very wrong. The results of bar polls provide an indicator of actual or prospective quality of performance, but such polls are also imperfect and generally receive little publicity. Newspaper endorsements may sway some voters, but endorsements of supreme court candidates are based largely on considerations such as a publisher's party leanings rather than simple assessment of candidates' merit (Suddes 2002).

This discussion provides a starting point for consideration of the impact that interest groups such as the business community can have in supreme court contests. Like other participants in campaigns, interest groups provide information directly to voters or stimulate the provision of information by others. The increased involvement of business groups and the pro-plaintiff groups in Ohio Supreme Court contests beginning in the mid-1980s produced what became permanent growth in the volume of campaign activity. In the period from 1974 to 1980, the mean level of combined spending by the two candidates in the general election period was about $185,000 in 2014 dollars.[4] In the period from 1984 to

2014, the mean in 2014 dollars was about $1.4 million, and no contest fell below $500,000. It should be kept in mind that the mean does not incorporate spending by party organizations and interest groups, including the substantial volume of independent spending by interest groups in the latter part of the period.

The most direct effect of such contributions and direct spending is simply to increase the volume of information about the candidates that is available to voters. That effect is magnified by news coverage of supreme court contests, which is largely a response to campaign activity. The greater the volume of that activity, the more coverage that newspapers and other news media devote to a contest (Baum and Klein 2007).

The potential impact of these higher levels of spending on voters' choices depends on both the volume of spending and the content of the messages that it funds. As to content, campaign messages in supreme court contests are often aimed at providing name recognition with a positive connotation, in forms such as family pictures or association of a candidate with a positive value such as experience or integrity. In states with nonpartisan ballots, such as Ohio, candidates and groups can engage in selective communication of a candidate's party affiliation to voters who are identified as supporters of that party. The Ohio parties themselves usually participate in that process by mailing sample ballots that include supreme court candidates.

The enhanced capacity to communicate to voters that higher spending allows could be used simply to reinforce these traditional efforts. As a result, more voters would become aware of candidates' names and party affiliations, resulting in reduced roll-off and higher levels of party-line voting. If one candidate had a substantial advantage in spending over the other, that advantage might translate into greater name recognition and awareness of the candidate's party affiliation from fellow party members, both of which would operate to increase the candidate's vote share.

Alternatively, a large portion of the communication that higher spending allows could be devoted to certain types of information that are usually hard to come by, such as candidates' positions on issues of judicial policy. Interest groups in Ohio might spur supreme court candidates to emphasize the tort issues that they care about or issues that they think might sway the voters. With the rise of independent group spending, groups can communicate those messages themselves. Either way, voters would have an increased opportunity to choose between candidates on the basis of their perceived stands on policy issues.

The volume of spending is important as well. As we discussed in chapter 2, even in the period that began in 1984 the scale of supreme court campaigns has varied a great deal. With mean spending per general election contest of about $1.4 million (in 2014 dollars) from 1984 to 2014, the standard deviation was about $950,000—and here too, if comprehensive data on independent spending were available, the variation would be even greater.

Of course, the more money spent in a contest, the more information can be communicated to voters. As a result, all of the potential effects of the higher spending levels since the mid-1980s are more likely to have occurred, and are likely to be much stronger, in some contests than in others.

In particular, campaigns with the highest levels of spending have the best chance to communicate information about certain issues of judicial policy to the voters. Even moderately large campaigns may be able to reach voters effectively with messages about criminal justice and other highly salient social issues, but economic issues such as torts are more difficult for campaigns to communicate effectively and for voters to assimilate. Thus, if Ohio Supreme Court candidates and their supporting groups include torts in their messages to voters, it is in the largest (and thus most visible) campaigns that voters have the best chance to make their decisions on the basis of that issue. As we discussed in chapter 2, torts did play a significant part in the contest between Alice Robie Resnick and Terrence O'Donnell in 2000 and in the two supreme court contests in 2002. The enhanced coverage of such large-scale campaigns by the news media also increased the chances that voters would learn about the candidates' stands on the issue that was responsible for the larger scale of supreme court contests from the mid-1980s on.

Because of these potential effects of the campaigns that were largest in scale, they merit consideration. Moreover, the attention that large-scale supreme court contests have received makes it valuable to understand how voters respond to the campaigns in those contests. But our central concern is explaining the outcomes of the full array of contests during our study period, especially the outcomes that ultimately moved the Ohio Supreme Court to a solid pro-defendant position.

Explaining Vote Shares

Since the middle of the twentieth century, the fortunes of the Ohio parties in supreme court elections have gone through three periods. In the period from 1950 through 1970, the Republican Party was dominant (Dubois 1980, 124). Democrats won five of twelve contested elections in the 1950s.[5] But that figure is deceptive: four of the Democratic victories were by incumbents who had sat on the court since the early 1930s, and the median Republican share of the vote was 63 percent. In the years from 1960 through 1970, Republicans won fourteen of sixteen contests.

From 1972 through 1982, in contrast, Democrats won eleven of seventeen contests. As in earlier periods, Democratic successes often reflected advantages based on incumbency or familiar names (Dubois 1980, 127; Lopeman 1999, 63). But also important were the increased efforts of the Ohio AFL-CIO and individual unions to elect candidates they favored, beginning in the mid-1970s (Barber 1984, 116; Tarr and Porter 1988, 131; Van Tine et al. 1998, 138–39). That record of success ultimately created the pro-plaintiff majority that upended long-standing rules favoring tort defendants. In turn, that shift in policy provided the stimulus for business groups to play a more active role in supreme court contests.

Since then, the Republicans have regained electoral dominance. In the 1984–2014 elections, Republican candidates won 78 percent of the thirty-seven contested elections, with a 75 percent success rate during the key period from 1984 through 2006. The median share of the vote that Republicans received during the full period was 55 percent.

As we have noted, however, two very successful Republican candidates established pro-plaintiff records as justices. Thus, it is more appropriate to categorize candidates based on their leanings in tort law, which we do in nearly all the analyses in this chapter. To do so, we eliminate all but one of the contests in which Republicans Andrew Douglas and Paul Pfeifer ran for seats on the court, since Douglas and Pfeifer might be perceived as similar to their Democratic opponents in their positions on tort law. This exception is the 1992 contest in which Pfeifer was opposed by the business community, a contest in which Democratic opponent Ronald Suster adopted the position of a pro-business candidate. Based on these amendments, pro-business candidates did not do quite as well as Republican candidates, but they still enjoyed a high success rate: 73 percent for the whole 1984–2014 period, 67 percent in the years from 1984 through 2006.

Still, pro-plaintiff candidates won a significant number of contests, and the shares of the votes that the two sides won varied a good deal. In the first stage of our inquiry, we probe the influence of business groups by analyzing the determinants of those vote shares. To gain a broader perspective, we extend that analysis back to 1980, to include two election years before the time that business became more active in supreme court elections and thus six contests in which Democratic candidates did very well (winning five of the six). Leaving aside seats for which one party did not run a candidate, our dependent variable is the proportion of the two-party vote that the pro-business candidate received.[6]

The pair of independent variables in which we are most interested concerns the scale of the campaigns on each side, measured by the amount of spending by the two candidates. There was a great deal of variation in spending among the pro-plaintiff candidates and among the pro-business candidates, just as there was in their combined spending. Not surprisingly, the two tended to covary, with a correlation of .651 across the 1980–2014 elections, but that correlation is far from perfect.

Pro-business candidates spent more money than their opponents in twenty-nine of the thirty-nine elections. The mean spending by pro-business candidates was about 45 percent higher than the mean for pro-plaintiff candidates. But there was a substantial change over time. In the 1980s and 1990s, the pro-business candidate spent more than the pro-plaintiff candidate in twelve of twenty-one contests; from 2000 to 2014, pro-business candidates spent more than their opponents in all but one of the eighteen contests.

Of course, not all spending is based on contributions from interest groups, but variation in the level of spending can be expected to track interest group activity rather well. From the late 1990s on, as we have noted, interest groups engaged in independent spending on behalf of candidates that is not reported and thus cannot be measured systematically.[7] That limitation requires some caution in interpreting the impact of candidate spending, especially because the two candidates' shares of total spending on their behalf may differ considerably from their shares of spending by the candidates themselves. In turn, analyses of the impact of candidate spending may underestimate the impact of money on election outcomes and voters' choices. But the candidates' spending is still a good general gauge of the scale of the campaigns.

There was a substantial relationship between the relative levels of spending between the two sides and their vote shares (r = .492), and pro-plaintiff candidates won much more often when they outspent their opponents (70%) than when they were outspent (24%).[8] In the great majority of contests, those in which the candidates do not emphasize substantive issues, the greatest impact of spending more than an opponent is probably an advantage in name recognition.[9] To get a more meaningful sense of the impact of spending and a more comprehensive picture of the determinants of outcomes, however, we need to take into account attributes of the candidates and the political environment.[10]

Perhaps the most important attribute of candidates is incumbency. In general, incumbents do well in elections. Certainly that has been true of the Ohio Supreme Court, at least for incumbents who had already won elections to the court (as distinguished from appointees running for the first time). Across the full 1980–2014 period, previously elected incumbents won twenty-two of twenty-five elections; in the critical 1984–2006 period, it was thirteen of fifteen. In the 1984–2006 period, when pro-plaintiff candidates won only eight of twenty-four elections, five of those victories came in the seven contests in which there were pro-plaintiff incumbents; the only two who suffered defeats (in 1984 and 1986) were the Celebrezze brothers, Frank and James.

One advantage of incumbents, including supreme court justices, is that they generally find it easier to raise money. In the set of supreme court contests we are analyzing, pro-business incumbents who had won previous supreme court elections outspent their opponents by more than a 2-1 margin on average. And even though pro-plaintiff candidates were generally at a financial disadvantage, the candidates on that side who were previously elected incumbents outspent their opponents by close to a 3-2 margin on average.

The change over time in the spending advantage between pro-plaintiff and pro-business candidates was largely a reflection of incumbency. In the 1980s and 1990s, pro-plaintiff incumbents who had won previous elections frequently appeared on the ballot, and seven of the nine pro-plaintiff candidates who had a spending advantage were incumbents. But Resnick in 2000 was the last pro-plaintiff incumbent to run in a contested race (Pfeifer had no opponent in 2004 and 2010), and pro-business candidates (ten of them elected incumbents) typically had large spending advantages over their opponents from 2002 on.

Our measures of spending by the two candidates incorporate this advantage of incumbency. But there is a second potential advantage of incumbency, one that rests on name recognition. Opportunities for justices to develop name recognition are not nearly as great as those for incumbents in many other offices (Barber 1984, 108, 110). Still, service on the court and presence on past ballots are likely to foster some name familiarity. To the extent that this is true, incumbency will produce higher vote shares even when spending is held constant.

Two other variables relate to favorable name recognition. One is a familiar political name. Of the names that have been familiar in Ohio politics at various times, supreme court candidates in the 1980–2014 period had two: Brown and Celebrezze.[11] We do not treat Celebrezze as a name that conferred an advantage on candidates because of the controversies in which the judicial Celebrezzes were involved; especially after 1982, having that name did not necessarily work in favor of a candidate. We do include Brown, though only on the plaintiff's side because there were no pro-business candidates named Brown.

The other recognition variable is whether a candidate on one side or the other had an Irish name because Irish names are thought to have positive connotations for Ohio voters (Ludlow 2015).[12] The validity of that impression is suggested by the highly improbable 2012 victory of William O'Neill, who was outspent by more than 100-to-1 and whose win (over an incumbent) broke a decade-long losing streak for Democratic supreme court candidates. That victory would seem to have no explanation other than O'Neill's Irish name and the name recognition he had developed in two unsuccessful races for supreme court seats.

The most relevant attribute of the political environment is the electoral strength of the candidate at the top of the ticket. That variable captures both the party loyalties of the voters who participated in supreme court contests, albeit imperfectly, and any coattail effects that might have occurred. To the extent that voters are aware of supreme court candidates' party affiliations or they can guess those affiliations from candidates' names, their vote for governor or president may be reflected in their supreme court votes.

The results of the first analysis, which includes all the eligible contests from 1980 through 2014, are shown in the first column of results in table 3.1. At least on the business side, an Irish name did seem to help. The relationship of more interest was the validation of a tendency for pro-plaintiff candidates to do better if they were incumbents, a relationship that held up even with controls for candidates' spending. Incumbency had no independent effect on the vote share for pro-business candidates. Nor, quite notably, did spending by either side have a significant impact once incumbency and other variables were taken into account.

The three contests in which Democrat O'Neill ran were anomalies, in that O'Neill raised and spent little money. As a result, those contests might distort the results. We analyzed the same model without those three contests; the results are shown in the second column of table 3.1. In this analysis, unlike the first analysis, all the variables are in the expected direction. But only spending and incumbency for the pro-plaintiff candidate were statistically significant at the conventional level.

We also used the same model to analyze the critical 1984–2006 period. The results, shown in the third column of table 3.1, are similar in most

TABLE 3.1. Determinants of the share of the two-party vote received by candidates with business support (regression coefficients)

VARIABLE	1980–2014 ALL CONTESTS	1980–2014 NO O'NEILL CANDIDACY	1984–2006 ALL CONTESTS	1984–2006 NO PRO-BUSINESS INCUMBENTS
Spending by pro-business candidate	−.003	.153	.064[b]	.135**
Spending by pro-plaintiff candidate	−.002	−.038*	−.008	−.064*
Pro-business incumbent	.025	.019	−.024	–
Pro-plaintiff incumbent	−.123**	−.096**	−.101*	−.043
Share of vote in top contest for pro-business candidate's party	.194	.153	.234	.305[c]
Pro-plaintiff candidate named Brown	−.034	−.007	.028	.075
Pro-business candidate with an Irish name	.076*	.055[a]	−.019	−.062
Pro-labor candidate with an Irish name	−.044	−.023	.013	.010
Number of contests	39	36	24	16

Notes: The three contests in which Justice Douglas ran for reelection and Justice Pfeifer's first election in 1992 are excluded from all analyses. Spending variables are the natural logs of spending by candidates on that side. Because all the relationships that achieved or came close to significance by the conventional standards were consistent with prior expectations, one-tailed tests of statistical significance were used.

** Significant at <.01 level.

* Significant at <.05 level.

[a] Significant at the .067 level.

[b] Significant at the .054 level.

[c] Significant at the .052 level.

respects. However, in contrast with the analysis for the longer period, spending by the business-backed candidate had a positive impact on that candidate's vote share, one that came very close to achieving statistical significance at the .05 level despite the smaller number of contests in the analysis.

Because the advantages of incumbency might obscure the effects of other factors in election outcomes, we conducted analyses of different sets of contests that were defined by incumbency status. The most striking pattern emerged for the contests without pro-business incumbents in the 1984–2006 period. That pattern is shown in the fourth column of table 3.1. For these contests, spending by each side had a significant impact on vote shares, despite the even smaller number of contests included in the analysis. However, incumbency for the pro-plaintiff candidate no longer had a significant impact. We need to be cautious in interpreting patterns that emerged from exploratory analyses, but these results provide some evidence that spending by each side made a substantial difference.

Significant though that last finding is, it captures the importance of spending on behalf of pro-business candidates only in part. At least as important were the overall levels of spending by candidates on the two sides across the period when election outcomes changed the supreme court's policies. During that period, as we have discussed, candidates supported by the business community had an advantage in spending far more often than not. And that advantage was most consistent and most substantial in the elections from 2002 on, when a pro-business majority on the court was established and solidified. It seems likely that a spending advantage made a difference in some of the victories for the business community during that period and earlier.

Analyzing Voters' Behavior

If the activity of business groups boosted the vote shares of the candidates they favored and helped to bring about their victories, one key question is how that happened. There are two possibilities, which are not mutually exclusive. Voters who were inclined to support pro-business candidates might have been mobilized disproportionately, or voters might have been moved to support pro-business candidates by their campaigns and the independent campaigns conducted on their behalf. In this section we examine these two possibilities.

PARTICIPATION AND ROLL-OFF

We begin our inquiry into voters' behavior with participation in supreme court contests. Starting with the assumption that few people go to the polls in order to vote in supreme court races, we focus on roll-off, the proportion of actual voters who did *not* cast ballots in a supreme court contest.

Roll-off is both substantial and variable. Over the forty-three contests for seats on the Ohio Supreme Court between 1980 and 2014, the mean roll-off was 22 percent. Roll-off rates varied from a low of 11 percent (the 1986 chief justice contest between Thomas Moyer and Frank Celebrezze) to a high of 32 percent (a 1980 contest for associate justice). The standard deviation was 4.6 percent.

Two questions about participation and roll-off are relevant to our concerns, each related to one of the general questions on which this chapter focuses. The first is whether there was a general advantage to pro-business candidates in the pattern of roll-off. If such an advantage existed, it would have contributed to the successes of most pro-business supreme court candidates during the study period. The second question is whether and how campaign activity by the two sides affected roll-off rates. Because much of our analysis of these questions concerns the attributes of individual voters, and because the surveys characterize voters in terms of partisan loyalties but not in terms of their positions on tort issues, we frequently focus on comparisons of Republican and Democratic voters. Of course, in the great majority of supreme court contests a pro-business Republican faced a pro-plaintiff Democrat, so that party and tort law positions coincided on the candidates' side.

We make extensive use of the voter surveys to analyze participation, so we should note at the outset that there are limits to what we can learn about roll-off from the surveys. Although survey respondents overstate their participation in presidential elections, they substantially understate their participation in supreme court contests (Adamany and Dubois 1975; Adamany and Shelley 1980). This understatement reflects the general lack of salience of those contests to voters: many people who voted for supreme court candidates simply do not remember that they did so. Our surveys showed substantial understatement, with mean actual participation of about 80 percent and mean reported participation of about 70 percent across the various contests in the survey years.[13] Thus our surveys cannot distinguish between participants and nonparticipants with anything like perfect accuracy. Still, they provide some information about the composition of the judicial electorate in high-visibility and lower-visibility contests.

On the question of whether pro-business candidates had a general advantage in participation, we can begin with the well-established finding that the rates at which eligible voters turn out at the polls increase with higher socioeconomic status (Flanigan et al. 2015, 74). There is some reason to expect a similar relationship for roll-off: among the people who do vote, those of higher status may be more likely to make choices for offices below the top levels and for ballot measures (Clubb and Traugott 1972, 144–46). This raises the possibility that roll-off (like turnout) generally favors Republican candidates and perhaps those with conservative issue positions (see Lewis-Beck et al. 2008, 97–99).

We probed the determinants of participation in each of the eighteen supreme court contests covered by our surveys, using variables whose potential importance was indicated by studies of election turnout (Rosenstone and Hansen 1993) and that were consistently available in the surveys. These variables included the strength of respondents' identifications with a political party, race and gender, level of education, and age. Labor union membership for the respondent or for any member of the respondent's family was included in the years for which it was available, all but 1988 and 1998. The only relationship that appeared in most contests was a tendency for participation to increase with age.[14]

The fact that education and race had no meaningful impact on roll-off suggests that there was no general advantage for pro-business candidates in patterns of participation. But we can probe that question more directly by comparing roll-off rates for voters who professed identification with a party or a leaning toward that party. In some individual contests, roll-off was appreciably higher for Democrats or for Republicans. But these differences balanced out across all the contests; the mean and median roll-off rates were quite similar for adherents to the two parties. Thus it does not appear that there was an overall advantage to candidates of either party (or to pro-business or pro-plaintiff candidates) in voter participation.

On the second question, the impact of campaign activity on roll-off rates, the first step is to ascertain the relationship between the level of activity (measured by spending) and voter participation. Higher spending, primarily a product of interest group contributions, makes more information available to voters. And as we have noted, a high volume of campaign activity triggers more extensive coverage of contests in the news media. One study found that spending levels did not affect participation in contests for intermediate appellate courts (Streb and Frederick 2011). But at the supreme court level, where levels of spending can reach much higher levels, there is strong evidence that the magnitude of spending affects participation (M. G. Hall and Bonneau 2008).

We address the relationship between spending and voter participation by analyzing the impact of spending alongside other attributes of the forty-three supreme court contests in the 1980–2014 period. Our measures of spending by the two sides are the same as in the analysis of vote shares. Three other variables are analogous to variables in that analysis: whether a previously elected incumbent was running, whether either candidate had a familiar political name, and whether either candidate had an Irish name.[15] Because a contest for chief justice might attract higher interest, we included that variable. Finally, there is good reason to expect

TABLE 3.2. Determinants of participation in supreme court contests, 1980–2014

VARIABLE	COEFFICIENT	STD. ERROR	SIGNIFICANCE
Spending by pro-business candidate	.020	.006	.002
Spending by pro-plaintiff candidate	.007	.003	.006
Gubernatorial	.035	.011	.002
Chief justice	.005	.017	.383
Familiar name	.040	.014	.005
Irish name	.025	.012	.027
Incumbent	.016	.012	.091
Constant	.383	.087	<.001

Notes: Participation is measured as the proportion of voters at the polls who voted in a contest. Spending is in 2014 dollars and is logged. "Gubernatorial" refers to years in which the governor (rather than the president) was elected. Incumbents are candidates who had previously been elected to the court. Significance levels are for one-tailed tests.

higher roll-off in presidential election years than in gubernatorial election years, simply because presidential elections attract more people with low levels of interest in politics (M. G. Hall and Bonneau 2008). Our dependent variable is the proportion of voters turning out at the polls who participated in a contest for the supreme court. The results of a model with all these variables are shown in table 3.2.

The impact of election timing is as expected: presidential elections bring out more voters with limited interest and knowledge of contests for lower-level offices. The impact of candidates' names is noteworthy in this context, because it underlines voters' reliance on information they can ascertain from the ballot in deciding whether to participate in supreme court contests. That impact also supports the conclusion that many voters do choose between supreme court candidates with little if any substantive knowledge of them.

Our primary interest, of course, is candidates' spending. Spending by each side had an impact that was highly significant and substantively meaningful, though not overwhelming. An increase from the median level of spending by the pro-business candidate across all contests to the median of the four contests with the highest spending levels by pro-business candidates was associated with a 2.0 percent increase in participation. For pro-plaintiff candidates, the analogous increase was 1.0 percent.[16]

The impact of spending is probably both direct and indirect. Campaign activity in forms such as the airing of television commercials gives voters more reason to participate in supreme court contests. That activity also stimulates news coverage of campaigns, coverage that reinforces the direct effects of campaign activity.

Thus it is clear that the volume of campaign activity affects voters' willingness to make choices in supreme court contests. But candidates do not seek to increase voter participation in itself; rather, they want to mobilize voters who are inclined to vote for them. For this reason, it is possible that if one candidate spends appreciably more than the other, roll-off will be lower for voters from the party of the advantaged candidate. Because the overall rates of roll-off for the two parties were about the same, we can address this question by looking at the correlation across contests between the balance of spending between the Republican and Democratic candidates and the balance of participation between Republican and Democratic voters. In other words, to what extent (if at all) did a candidate's advantage in spending translate into an advantage in mobilizing party voters?

As it turned out, the correlation was very low—.002.[17] As that low correlation suggests, there were several contests in the survey years in which the party of the candidate who spent more money actually had a higher rate of roll-off. That was true, for instance, of the two high-profile contests in which James and Frank Celebrezze were candidates in 1984 and 1986.

However, it is worth noting the pattern for the 2002 contests, the ones that featured an extraordinary level of campaign activity and in which the outcomes established a pro-business majority on the court. The Republican pro-business candidates outspent their Democratic opponents, and—with the considerable help of independent groups—they had a sizeable advantage in spending for television commercial time (Goldberg et al. 2002, 32). They also had an advantage in roll-off: the rates for Democratic voters were 3.6 percentage points higher in the Janet Burnside–Evelyn Stratton contest and 6.0 percent higher in the Tim Black–Maureen O'Connor contest. These differences did not necessarily reflect the larger size of the Republican campaigns, and in themselves they could not account for the Republican victories; Stratton won by 11 percentage points and O'Connor by 14. But they may have been a contributing factor.

It is worth reiterating that the failure of some voters to remember that they voted in supreme court contests complicates any effort to trace patterns of roll-off. With that caveat, we have found clear evidence that the level of campaign activity affected voters' choices whether to participate in those contests. The fact that increases in spending by the business community had greater impact on those choices suggests the possibility that pro-business candidates gained an advantage from higher spending levels. There is also suggestive evidence that in the 2002 contests, the candidates favored by the business community gained some advantage from differential roll-off rates. On the whole, however, it appears that neither pro-business nor pro-plaintiff candidates benefited substantially from roll-off rates. If higher levels of spending gave candidates an advantage, as indicated by our analysis of vote shares in table 3.1, that advantage seems to have come primarily from influencing voters' choices between supreme court candidates rather than their decisions whether to cast a vote in supreme court contests. We turn next to these choices.

CHOOSING BETWEEN CANDIDATES

To probe the impact of campaign spending and other factors on voters' choices between candidates, once again we use the surveys of voters. We aggregate survey responses across all the contests in which business groups and pro-plaintiff groups were on opposite sides so that we can take into account attributes of both voters and the contests in which they cast votes.

In our analysis of the combined surveys, the unit of analysis is a voter's choice between candidates in a specific contest. Consistent with our contest-level analysis, we code our dependent variable as whether a voter chose the candidate supported by business groups in that contest or the candidate supported by pro-plaintiff groups. Two of the contests that we dropped from the contest-level analysis (the contests in which Douglas ran in 1984 and 1990) fell in our survey years, and they were dropped from this analysis as well.

Our independent variables include attributes of election contests and of individual voters. The attributes of contests are the same as those included in the contest-level analysis of vote shares earlier in this chapter. The individual attributes are as follows:

party identification, on a 5-point scale[18]
ideological identification, on a 5-point scale[19]
sex
racial identification, dichotomized as white and nonwhite
level of education
age

These variables are coded so that positive coefficients mean that the business-supported candidate was more likely to receive votes from voters of that candidate's own party, conservatives, men, whites, people with more education, and older people—the relationships that we probably would expect. The results are shown in table 3.3. Because our analysis includes attributes of both individuals and contests, we employ a multi-level regression technique.[20]

We can start with the impact of campaign spending. Spending by the candidate who received support from the business community had a strong positive relationship with votes for that candidate. Spending by the pro-plaintiff candidate had a negative relationship with votes for the pro-business candidate, although one that was considerably weaker and not statistically significant.

One way to think about the impact of spending by the pro-business candidate is in partisan terms. As table 3.3 shows, and as we will discuss shortly, there is a strong relationship between voters' party identifications and their votes in supreme court contests. Setting aside the 1998 contest in which the pro-plaintiff candidate (Paul Pfeifer) was a Republican, the impact of spending by the pro-business candidate can be gauged in terms of defection rates of Democratic and Republican voters. Across the fifteen contests in which neither Pfeifer nor Douglas was a candidate, there was a correlation of .406 between Republican spending and the proportion of Democrats who voted for the pro-business candidate; there was a correlation of -.809 between Republican spending and the proportion of Republicans who voted for the pro-plaintiff candidate. Thus the volume of spending by pro-business candidates seemed to have considerable impact on their ability to win Democratic votes and an even greater impact on their ability to hold on to Republican votes.

The findings for other variables are of interest for what they tell us about the bases for voters' choices between candidates. Incumbency for the pro-plaintiff candidate had a strong relationship with votes for that candidate. That finding is consistent with what we found in the analysis of vote shares in table 3.1, and it is noteworthy once again that incumbency enhanced the positions of pro-plaintiff candidates even with controls for spending levels. Thus we have additional evidence for the conclusion that the series of election outcomes suggests: it was largely the advantages of incumbency that slowed the development of a pro-business majority on the court.

Surprisingly, incumbency for the pro-business candidate also had a strong negative relationship with votes for the pro-business candidate. That negative relationship was a product of the fact that incumbents on

TABLE 3.3. Determinants of votes for business-supported candidate, combined surveys

VARIABLE	COEFFICIENT.	STD. ERROR	SIGNIFICANCE
Contest level			
Spending by pro-business candidate	1.089	.301	<.001
Spending by pro-plaintiff candidate	–.068	.053	.200
Pro-business incumbent	–.711	.383	.063
Pro-plaintiff incumbent	–.780	.328	.017
Vote share for pres/gov candidate from party of pro-plaintiff candidate	2.882	1.258	.022
Pro-plaintiff candidate named Brown	.655	.622	.292
Pro-business candidate with an Irish name	–.973	.589	.098
Pro-plaintiff candidate with an Irish name	.926	.474	.051
Individual level			
Party identification	.448	.031	<.001
Ideological identification	.116	.034	.001
Gender	–.076	.079	.334
Race	–.004	.012	.719
Education	.134	.036	<.001
Age	.005	.003	.038
Constant	–17.395	4.260	<.001

Notes: Natural logs of spending amounts are used. Incumbents are those who had won previous supreme court elections. Significance levels are for two-tailed tests.

the pro-business side spent considerably more money than other pro-business candidates. When pro-business spending is removed from the analysis, the negative relationship disappears. However, incumbency status for the pro-business candidate still had no positive effect on votes for that candidate.

At the individual level, party identification, ideological identification, and education all had strong relationships with the vote: pro-business candidates did better among Republicans, conservatives, and highly educated people. The impact of party identification in Ohio's officially nonpartisan elections underlines the ability of some voters to discern information about candidates' party affiliations even when the ballot does not identify those affiliations as well as the willingness of at least some voters to act on that information.

It is noteworthy that ideological identifications have a significant statistical impact on voters' choices between candidates even with party identifications in the equation. The statistical impact of education might reflect the impact of economic status, which correlates highly with education.[21]

Estimated probabilities of voters' choices between candidates under different conditions cannot be calculated from the multilevel statistical routine that we use. For that reason, we also analyze a logistic regression model that includes only the individual-level variables, one in which the findings for those variables are similar to those in the multilevel model. The estimated effects of party, ideology, and education are of interest.[22] With the other variables set at their median values, strong Democrats were more likely than strong Republicans to vote for the pro-plaintiff candidate by 39 percentage points. Strong Democrats who were also strong liberals were more likely than their conservative Republican counterparts to vote for a pro-plaintiff candidate by 48 percentage points. And when education is added to the mix (with high-school graduates on the liberal Democratic side and college graduates on the conservative Republican side), the difference increases to 53 percentage points.

In the discussion of participation, we asked whether Democratic voters rolled off at a higher rate than Republicans, thereby giving an advantage to Republican supreme court candidates. Here we can ask an analogous question about partisan voting: were Democratic voters more likely to defect from their parties' candidates than Republicans? Across the eighteen contests covered by the surveys, the mean defection rate was 10 percentage points higher for Democratic voters; the median was 8 percentage points higher. If we exclude the three contests in which Douglas or Pfeifer was the Republican candidate, the mean is 2 percentage points higher for Democrats, the median 4 percentage points higher.

The election years in which surveys were conducted are not necessarily representative of the full study period. However, the results for those years indicate that Republican candidates' success stemmed in part from their doing better than Democratic candidates in winning votes from people who identified with a candidate's party. However, that advantage was fairly small when the relatively liberal (and popular) Republicans were not candidates.[23]

Our findings for those individual attributes have implications for voters' intentions when they cast their votes in supreme court contests. We turn next to that issue.

What Voters Wanted

As we showed in chapter 1, Ohio voters shaped and reshaped the tort policies of the Ohio Supreme Court through their collective choices between competing candidates for the court. The defeats of James Celebrezze in 1984 and Frank Celebrezze in 1986, and to a lesser degree the election of Herbert Brown in 1986, moved the court away from its strong liberalism. The elections of 1988 and 1992 brought in three new justices who strongly favored tort plaintiffs and thereby shifted the court to the left. The 2002 election of Maureen O'Connor decisively moved the court rightward again, and the elections of Judith Lanzinger and Robert Cupp in the two election years that followed consolidated the gains of the business community by establishing a strong conservative majority on the court. That majority remains solid today, and it is likely to continue well into the future.

To what extent did voters act deliberately to achieve these outcomes—and especially the establishment of a firmly rooted pro-business majority on the court after 2000? At one end of the spectrum, we could imagine that a large portion of the electorate understood the stakes for tort law in elections to the supreme court and chose candidates largely on that basis. As a result, the shifts in the court's positions in tort law could be said to reflect the public will. At the other end, we could imagine that very few voters were aware of those stakes and that they chose between competing candidates on the basis of criteria which had little substantive meaning. In this section we examine evidence about where the voters stood on that spectrum.

The first requisite for voters to act deliberately on the basis of their views about tort policies is that they know the consequences of their choices. In most of the supreme court contests since 1980, as we discussed in chapter 2, potential voters received little or no information about the candidates' positions in tort law. In some election years, a careful newspaper reader might have seen stories with information related to those positions, such as the positions of interest groups concerned with torts. In other election years, even those hints were absent.

The contests in 2000 and 2002 were sharp exceptions, because candidates and groups sponsored a large volume of television commercials related to tort issues. The heavily funded campaign by business groups against Alice Robie Resnick in 2000 attacked her for her ties with trial lawyers. In the two contests of 2002, supporters of the Republican candidates pointed to what they saw as serious problems resulting from medical malpractice issues, and Democrat Tim Black criticized his opponent Maureen O'Connor on the ground that she was close to insurance companies and doctors.

Individual tort decisions and decisional trends in the supreme court also get some attention in Ohio media. Indeed, the court's 1999 decision striking down a sweeping "tort reform" statute received front-page coverage in Ohio's major newspapers.[24] But that was an exceptional case. An Ohioan who was an assiduous reader of the newspapers and other Ohio news media might have gained a sense of the positions of individual justices in tort law, but the task would not have been easy.

Of particular interest are the justices who diverged to some degree from the general tendency of Democrats to take pro-plaintiff positions and Republicans to take pro-business positions in tort law. When the unknown Democrat Herbert Brown was elected to the court, voters had no basis for predicting that he would not take a clear pro-plaintiff position once he joined the court. In contrast, when Republicans Andrew Douglas and Paul Pfeifer first won their seats on the court (in 1984 and 1992, respectively), a careful and astute voter might have learned of Douglas's ties to the labor movement and Pfeifer's experience as a trial lawyer and inferred that they would take pro-plaintiff positions in tort law. But that would not have been easy.

It is more plausible that Ohioans gradually learned of Douglas's and Pfeifer's records of liberalism in tort law as justices.[25] Douglas ran for reelection after six and twelve years on the court. Pfeifer ran for reelection three times, though only after his first term did he face an opponent. In that election his Democratic opponent took a pro-business position, thereby reversing the usual sides. In light of Pfeifer's judicial record and this reversal, it seems likely that at least some voters learned of his pro-plaintiff stance.

Some of the post-election surveys provide direct evidence about what voters knew about the candidates, including information related to tort policy. One was the 2006 survey. As we have noted, the election of Republican Robert Cupp to succeed the retiring Democrat Alice Robie Resnick replaced a strongly pro-plaintiff justice with a strongly pro-defendant justice and thereby strengthened the conservative majority that had been established in 2002. The reelection of Republican Terrence O'Donnell over Democrat William O'Neill maintained the status quo, but an O'Neill victory likely would have shored up the liberal minority on the court.

O'Neill spent little money, but the other three candidates were fairly well funded. In the contest between Cupp and Ben Espy, the two candidates spent about $1.4 million in 2014 dollars. In addition, a little over $1 million was spent on television advertising by outside groups in the two contests. Although the 2006 contests are not among those that could be classified as highly visible, the candidates and their supporters had a good opportunity to communicate with the voters. But tort issues were essentially invisible in the campaigns, so voters would have had to act independently to take those issues into account in their choices.

The 2006 survey of Ohio voters showed that most had learned little about the candidates by the time they cast their ballots. Of particular interest is a question directly relevant to tort issues. Voters in each contest were asked which candidate, if either, was supported by labor unions. Voters who knew the candidates' party affiliations might infer labor support from those affiliations, and indeed there was a strong relationship between possession of one piece of information and the other. For that reason, correct answers hardly guaranteed that voters were aware of the stakes of the election for tort policy. But the level of voters' knowledge tells us something about the likelihood of such awareness: someone who recognized the potential impact of the outcome for tort policy could be expected to know which side unions were on.

From this perspective, the results are striking. Of the respondents who reported voting in the O'Donnell-O'Neill contest, 16 percent said that O'Neill was supported by labor, compared with 10 percent who cited O'Donnell. The remaining 74 percent did not offer an answer. We think it reasonable to assume that those voters did not know the answer to the question, especially because the great majority explicitly said that they did not know. Of those who did answer, undoubtedly some were guessing. To take guessing into account, we can estimate the level of voter knowledge by subtracting the percentage of wrong answers from the percentage of rights answers. Thus the estimated level of knowledge on this question was 16 percent minus 10 percent, or 6 percent. We follow the same approach on other questions about voter knowledge.

In the Cupp-Espy contest too, 16 percent gave the right answer—that Espy was supported by labor. In contrast with the other contest, only 2 percent gave the wrong answer. Thus the estimated knowledge level was 14 percent—better than in the O'Donnell-O'Neill contest, but still not very high. In neither case does it appear that information related to the policy stakes in that contest was widespread.

The 1990 contests provide another perspective. Republicans Andrew Douglas and Craig Wright were both running for reelection. Their levels of campaign funding were similar to those in 2006. Stuart Banks, who challenged Douglas, was poorly funded. Wright's Democratic challenger, Stephanie Tubbs Jones, was better funded, though Wright still had a substantial advantage. To a degree, the relatively low levels of campaign funding and news coverage probably reflected an expectation that Wright and Douglas would win easily. As it turned out, Douglas won nearly three-quarters of the vote, but the Jones-Wright contest was quite close. As in 2006, tort issues played no visible role in the campaigns.

In the 1990 post-election survey, respondents were asked several questions about the candidates, including their ideological positions, their positions on government regulation of business, and whether they were close to unions or business. Across these questions, voters' levels of knowledge were uniformly low.

A matter of particular interest was whether voters differentiated between Wright, an orthodox conservative, and Douglas, who had begun to anger fellow Republicans with relatively liberal positions on tort law during his first term on the court. On the ideology question, 17 percent of voters identified Wright as conservative and 3 percent as liberal. For Douglas, the split was similar—20 percent to 5 percent. On business regulation, with its implications for tort law, few voters identified either Wright or Douglas with a position, and in both instances about twice as many voters identified the justice as anti-regulation than as pro-regulation. The business and union closeness items are interesting because of Douglas's ties to labor unions. Seventeen percent of voters identified him as really close to unions, compared with 12 percent for Wright. But 23 percent identified Douglas as really close to business, compared with 17 percent for Wright. The general lack of knowledge of Douglas's distinctive position is quite understandable, given the limited information available to voters. But that lack of knowledge strongly suggests a low awareness of tort issues among voters in most Ohio contests.

The four high-visibility contests that took place in years in which voter surveys were conducted were the Celebrezze contests in 1984 and 1986 and the two contests in 2002. In 1984 and 1986, contributors to the competing candidates were motivated primarily by the tort issues that had become prominent with the court's sharp move to the left, but those issues played a meaningful role in only the 1986 contest. In both contests the focus was on the qualifications and conduct of the Celebrezze brothers, and that focus was undoubtedly the primary reason for their defeat.

The 1984 and 1986 surveys asked voters about the reasons for their choices. Questions about such reasons have serious limitations, because people are not very good at recalling and articulating why they made a particular choice when they faced a decision of some type.[26] However, these questions provide a window on what voters were thinking about.

In both election years, the great majority of voters gave reasons for their choices. The reasons they offered ranged widely, but in each contest the largest number referred to negative feelings about the incumbent and the second largest number referred to the candidates' party affiliations. In 1984, a sprinkling of responses in the James Celebrezze–Craig Wright contest—by a very generous interpretation of the responses, 7.5 percent—related to judicial policy in one way or another: the court's visible role in partial refunds of utility charges to consumers, ideology, unspecified issue positions, and union endorsements.[27] It is quite possible that some of these voters had tort issues in mind. But if so, they were a very small number.

In 1986, voters were given a chance to offer as many as three reasons for their choice. Nearly everyone offered a first reason in the Frank Celebrezze–Thomas Moyer contest, and about 15 percent had a second reason. In this contest too, only a small proportion of responses were related to judicial policy. By the same very generous interpretation used in the 1984 contest, the proportion of voters who offered responses related to judicial policy was almost exactly the same, 7.5 percent.[28] It is noteworthy that this proportion was no higher than in the 1984 contest, in light of the higher level of publicity in 1986 and the chance for voters to offer multiple reasons for their votes. A single Moyer voter cited tort policy directly, saying that Celebrezze had hurt the insurance business. The same number of voters reported voting for Celebrezze after picking his name out of a hat.

In light of the content of the campaigns, it would have been surprising if tort issues had been on many voters' minds in 1984, 1990, and 2006. Arguably, the same was true of 1986, because the campaign was dominated by questions about the conduct of Chief Justice Celebrezze. The election in 2002 was different because torts played a prominent role in the two very well-funded campaigns for the supreme court contests that year. Certainly a reasonably attentive voter could discern that the outcomes of the two contests would have a significant impact on personal injury law. Two questions about the candidates, one in each contest, provide some sense of how well the differences between the candidates were communicated to the voters.

In the contest between Republican Evelyn Stratton and Democrat Janet Burnside, voters were asked about the candidates' ideological positions. Burnside was identified as liberal by 17 percent, as moderate by 14 percent, and as conservative by 3 percent. Stratton was identified as liberal by 6 percent, as moderate by 19 percent, and as conservative by 28 percent. Altogether, 10 percent identified Burnside as liberal and Stratton as conservative, and an additional 13 percent put Burnside in a more liberal category than Stratton.

In the contest between Republican Maureen O'Connor and Democrat Tim Black, voters were asked whether each candidate was supported by labor unions, business, both, or neither. Leaving aside the "both" category, 19 percent of the voters cited union support for Black, 3 percent business support. For O'Connor, the figures were 6 percent union and 19 percent business. Altogether, 10 percent of the voters cited both union support for Black and business support for O'Connor.

These findings do not directly address voters' awareness that their collective choices would affect tort policy in Ohio, and responses to the questions about labor and business support for the candidates undoubtedly were affected by some voters' knowledge of the candidates' party affiliations. Still, the responses indicate that meaningful proportions of the voters had gained a sense of policy-relevant differences between the candidates, most likely as a result of the television advertising in the 2002 contests. That indication is important, because the victories of the two Republican candidates established the pro-business majority that has continued since that time. Did a subset of the voters who may have understood the stakes in the outcome of the supreme court contests for tort policy actually determine that outcome?

To address that question, we analyzed the relationship between voters' knowledge of policy-relevant information and party-line voting. In both contests, but especially in the Stratton-Burnside contest, we found that knowledgeable voters (those who were correct on interest group support for O'Connor and Black and those who rated Burnside as more liberal than Stratton) were more likely to vote for their own party's candidate than were other voters.[29]

In 2002, the respondents who voted in the supreme court contests leaned Republican in their party identifications by a 15 percentage point margin in the Black-O'Connor contest and by an 11 percent margin in the Burnside-Stratton contest. That skew probably reflected the disproportionate turnout of Republicans in what was a very good year for Republican candidates who ran statewide. If policy-related knowledge of the candidates enhanced partisan voting, then it might be that knowledgeable voters swung the balance in one or both of the contests.

The evidence strongly suggests that this did not occur in the Black-O'Connor contest. Even though knowledgeable Republicans had disproportionately strong party identifications, they were no more likely than other Republicans to vote for O'Connor. (The overall relationship between knowledge and partisan voting in that contest resulted from the effect of knowledge on Democratic voters.)

The picture is not as stark in the Burnside-Stratton contest, because Republicans who knew that Burnside was more liberal than Stratton were considerably more likely to vote for Stratton than were other Republicans; the rates were, respectively, 95 percent and 66 percent. But that difference was counteracted by a similar difference for Democratic voters, and Democrats were slightly more likely to be knowledgeable than Republicans. Moreover, the knowledgeable Republicans were much more likely than other Republicans to be strong party identifiers and strong conservatives. Even without taking that fact into account, the best estimate of the net effect of knowledge of the candidates' ideological positions is about zero.[30]

We can gain another perspective by examining patterns of partisan voting. Philip Dubois (1980, chap. 3) and Herbert Kritzer (2015, chap. 6) analyzed the county-level correlations between the vote for supreme court candidates and for gubernatorial candidates as a way to gauge the extent of party-line voting in the supreme court contests. Although these correlations do not capture individual-level behavior directly, variation in the strength of the correlations across contests tends to reflect the degree of party-line voting at the individual level (Kritzer 2015, 175). Not surprisingly, both scholars found that the average strength of the correlations is weaker in Ohio than in states with purely partisan elections and stronger than in states with purely nonpartisan elections. As we would also expect, there is greater variation in the correlations from election to election in Ohio (and in other states with nonpartisan ballots) than in the states with purely partisan elections.

Consistent with the Dubois and Kritzer findings, the surveys of Ohio voters show a substantial degree of party-line voting for supreme court candidates, though distinctly lower than in voting for partisan offices and in voting for the Ohio Supreme Court when respondents were told the candidates' party affiliations (Klein and Baum 2001). There was also considerable variation in the extent of party-line voting across contests, variation that correlates with the scale of campaigns (Rock and Baum 2010).

In order to include all the supreme court contests between 1980 and 2014, we use Kritzer's data to analyze the relationship between the extent of party-line voting and attributes of the candidates and contests that might enhance or limit partisan voting. The attribute in which we are most interested is the presence of Paul Pfeifer or Andrew Douglas on the ballot as an incumbent. Did enough voters know that Pfeifer and Douglas had proved to be relatively liberal and act on that knowledge to weaken the relationship between party identification and the vote?

Because of the evidence that partisan voting increases with the visibility of supreme court contests in Ohio, we include variables for the spending levels of the Republican and Democratic candidates. And because the identification of a candidate as African American could serve as a cue to voters, in part as an indication of the candidate's ideological position (McDermott 1998), we include variables for the presence of a Democratic or Republican African American in the contest. The results are shown in table 3.4.

Aside from the variable of greatest interest, two other results are noteworthy. The level of Republican spending had a highly significant impact on the degree of partisan voting; the level of Democratic spending did not. A Republican African American candidate weakened partisan voting, but a Democratic African American candidate did not. This result suggests that black Republican candidates reduced party-line voting by attracting votes from black Democrats, by triggering expectations that black candidates from either party are liberals, or both.

Despite the small number of contests in which Pfeifer or Douglas ran as a sitting judge, there was a significant negative relationship between their presence on the ballot and the extent of partisan voting.[31] In contrast with our survey findings in Douglas's 1990 contest, this relationship is consistent with the possibility that enough voters knew of these two

TABLE 3.4. Determinants of levels of partisan voting in supreme court contests, 1980–2014

VARIABLE	COEFFICIENT	STD. ERROR	SIGNIFICANCE
Pfeifer/Douglas	–.223	.094	.023
Black Democrat	–.006	.084	.941
Black Republican	–.292	.120	.020
Spending by Republican	.083	.029	.007
Spending by Democrat	–.012	.011	.273
Constant	–.343	.385	.378

Notes: Significance levels are for two-tailed tests. "Pfeifer/Douglas" refers to contests in which either justice ran as an incumbent.

justices' departures from the usual positions of Republican justices and acted on that knowledge to weaken the linkage between party and the vote.[32] However, these were not the contests in which the correlation between gubernatorial and supreme court voting was weakest; they were ranked 34th through 36th among the forty-three contests. Ranking below them were, among others, the two contests with African American Republican candidates and the two contests in the 1980s with Democrats named Brown—traditionally identified as a Republican name in Ohio politics (Barber 1971, 777n61; Dubois 1980, 83–84).

Ultimately, what counted the most in the Douglas and Pfeifer reelection bids was the weakness of the campaigns by their opponents, who could not garner substantial contributions from the usual sources of funding for Democratic supreme court candidates. Douglas won 73 percent of the vote in 1990 and 66 percent in 1996. Pfeifer received 71 percent in 1998, and in the two elections that followed (not included in our analysis) he ran unopposed. Even if some voters' awareness of their relative liberalism was a net advantage for Douglas and Pfeifer, that advantage was hardly necessary for them to retain their seats on the court.

The evidence on voters' intentions is both complex and mixed in its implications. Taken as a whole, the evidence points firmly against the conception that the shifts in the supreme court's balance between pro-plaintiff and pro-business justices reflected deliberate choices by voters. In light of the limited volume of relevant information available to voters in the great majority of elections, it seems effectively impossible for more than a small portion of those voters to recognize the stakes in supreme court contests for tort policy. The survey data verify that impression.

There are some signs that enough voters gained an impression of candidates' ideological positions to potentially affect some election outcomes. But even under the most favorable conditions for such an effect, in 2002, the evidence indicates that this was not the case. Moreover, acting on an impression of ideological positions is some distance from acting deliberately to shape tort policy.

We did find that there was a fairly strong relationship between voters' party identifications and their votes in supreme court contests, a relationship that strengthened in the more visible contests. Moreover, ideology and education (which captures economic status to a considerable degree) had their own impact on the vote. To some extent, then, voters' general political attitudes and interests helped determine the outcomes of supreme court contests and thus the court's direction in tort policy.

But that is not the same thing as intending to shape judicial policy on torts in particular ways. At the elite level, tort law was the dominant issue motivating interest group involvement in supreme court elections. At the mass level, that issue appears to have had little impact on voters' individual and collective choices between candidates. If the consequences of those collective choices were described to voters, some would be pleased and others would be dismayed. It seems likely that the overwhelming majority would be surprised.

Why Did Business Win?

Our findings in this chapter tell us something about the determinants of voter participation and voter choices between candidates in supreme court elections at the individual level as well as the determinants of election outcomes. They also offer insight into the impact on voters of the highly visible supreme court contests that have become more common in the current era. But our central concern is the sources of the ultimate success of the business community in winning a court that is relatively favorable to its interests. If that success cannot be ascribed to voters' views about tort policy, where does the explanation lie?

One way to think about this question is in terms of nonpartisan elections in general. Some scholars have argued that Republican candidates have an inherent advantage in elections in which the candidates' party affiliations are not on the ballot.[33] That advantage might stem from attributes of the candidates and campaigns, especially Republican advantages in resources with which to get their messages out in a nonpartisan environment (Hawley 1973). Alternatively, the higher socioeconomic status of Republicans in the mass public might lead to higher participation and greater awareness of the candidates' party affiliations in nonpartisan elections.

The empirical evidence for the possibility of an inherent Republican advantage in nonpartisan elections is mixed, but it merits consideration. That is especially true because the leading student of Ohio judicial elections, writing in the 1970s and 1980s, perceived a distinct Republican advantage under the nonpartisan ballot (Barber 1971; Barber 1984, 113–14, 119). Moreover, it is noteworthy that in the current era, Republican candidates for the supreme court do somewhat better on average than the Republicans who run in partisan elections for president or governor in the same years. The mean proportion of the two-party vote won by Republican supreme court candidates in the 1980–2014 elections was 3.7 percent higher than their party colleagues at the top of the ticket. This was enough to make a difference in several contests, though that was true of only one contest after 2000, the period in which the court's pro-business majority was established and strengthened.

Of course, partisan lines on the Ohio Supreme Court have not coincided with divisions in tort law. The development of a pro-business majority was delayed for considerable time by the presence of one or two pro-plaintiff Republicans on the court from 1985 on. But Republican candidates for the court achieved a high enough level of success that the court eventually gained a pro-business majority despite that obstacle.

On the voters' side, as we discussed earlier, Republican candidates did not enjoy a general advantage in roll-off in the years in which surveys were conducted, though differential participation by Republican and Democratic voters may have provided some benefit to Republican candidates. Republicans did have an advantage in winning votes from adherents to the other party. Although that advantage was small when contests with the pro-plaintiff Republicans are excluded, the Republican advantage in defections probably was larger in election years in which there were no surveys.[34]

Did this difference reflect differential knowledge of which candidate was Democratic and which was Republican? In three election years, survey respondents were asked questions relating to candidates' party affiliations. In three contests in 1988 and 1994, they were asked to identify the party of the two competing candidates; in two 2006 contests, they were asked which candidate was the Democrat. On the whole, Democratic and Republican voters did about equally well, suggesting that there was no Republican advantage in knowledge of candidates' party affiliations.

But another type of evidence suggests otherwise. In five contests in 1994, 1998, and 2002, some respondents were asked how they voted without being given the candidates' party affiliations while others were told those affiliations. In each contest the Democratic candidate did better when party information was provided, with a mean gain of 9 percent and a median of 8 percent. It is uncertain which type of evidence should be given more weight, so there is no clear conclusion.

If we shift our attention to the candidates and campaigns, the most important fact is the advantage of pro-business candidates in the amount of money they could spend during campaigns. That advantage was only moderate in the 1980s and 1990s, because of the several contests in which pro-plaintiff justices who had won previous supreme court elections enjoyed an advantage in spending. The spending advantage of pro-business candidates was overwhelming from 2002 through 2014, a period in which no pro-plaintiff incumbent ran for reelection.[35]

As we have shown, there was not a clear and consistent relationship between spending by the two sides and the outcomes of elections to the Ohio Supreme Court. However, we found considerable evidence that spending makes a difference. Whatever else campaign spending accomplishes, it is a means to enhance favorable name recognition for candidates. That function is especially important in contests below the top levels. Thus, it seems likely that the spending advantage of groups that favored a pro-defendant position in tort law played a substantial part in the eventual creation of a majority for that position on the supreme court.

We should emphasize that it is impossible to specify with any precision the effects of campaign spending on election outcomes and thus on judicial policy in Ohio. The available evidence on both spending and other potential determinants of election outcomes is too limited and too complex to allow firm conclusions. For example, we cannot measure the impact of the tendency for Ohio newspapers to endorse Republican supreme court candidates (Suddes 2002) or of the news stories in 1984 and 1986 that painted a highly negative picture of the Celebrezze brothers during their unsuccessful campaigns for reelection (see Tarr and Porter 1988, 174–76). What we *can* say with some confidence is that the mobilization of the business community to reverse an unfavorable trend in the tort policies of the Ohio Supreme Court was one key element in the process by which the election process brought about that reversal.

FOUR

Findings and Implications

In the preceding three chapters we undertook a broad examination of election campaigns, voting behavior, and judicial decisions for the Ohio Supreme Court. Our aim was to understand the linkages among them and thereby to gain a better sense of the relationship between judicial elections and public policy.

We begin this conclusion by summarizing and pulling together our findings. We then turn to implications of what we found for our understanding of judicial elections and for evaluation of judicial elections as an institution. Whether one views the findings positively or as cause for concern likely depends on normative views regarding the practice of electing judges.

Findings

Tort law is one of the most important fields of activity for state supreme courts. The decisions that supreme courts reach and the legal rules they make have a major impact on people who suffer injuries and on individuals and institutions that might be held responsible for these injuries. The significance of supreme courts' role in tort law is highlighted when courts issue major decisions that establish the balance between plaintiffs and defendants on a consequential issue.

Over the four decades covered in this study, the most prominent attribute of tort policy in the Ohio Supreme Court was its volatility. The proportions of decisions won by plaintiffs and defendants and the tenor of the legal doctrines promulgated by the court fluctuated a great deal before they settled into a pro-defendant theme that now seems likely to continue for some time.

By no means was that fluctuation random. Rather, it resulted primarily from changes in the membership of the court. Individual justices differed widely in their positions on tort law issues, and the replacement of sitting justices with new justices who had quite different positions brought about the shifts in tort policy that occurred over the years. In some instances this change was fairly abrupt, but in others court policy on torts changed more slowly over a period of time.

Some new justices joined the court as a result of interim appointments by governors, but those justices needed to win elections early in their tenure to remain on the court (and several did not). Most justices joined the court by winning elections. Thus it was ultimately Ohio's voters who brought about the changes in the court's tort policies that occurred over the years. In the early to mid-1980s, the voters acted to remove four sitting justices from office, two of them recent appointees. But incumbent justices then enjoyed a long winning streak, one that lasted from 1988 through 2010. During that period it was the voters' choices in open-seat contests that moved the court in one direction or the other and that ultimately brought about the court's current pro-defendant stance.

Both the plaintiffs and defendants in tort cases are diverse groups. But tort policy is largely a clash between individuals and institutions in business and government—each represented by a segment of the bar. In practice, the primary groups that support the interests of plaintiffs are labor unions and the trial lawyers who represent plaintiffs. On the other side is the business community, including professionals such as medical doctors. Insurance companies, which typically pay the damages awarded to plaintiffs in court or agreed upon in out-of-court settlements, are especially prominent on the defense side.

The high stakes of the two sides in tort policy are reflected in the efforts that each devotes to winning more favorable policy in the legislative and judicial branches of state government. Those efforts include activity in supreme court campaigns. This activity consists primarily of financial contributions to candidates and their parties and, increasingly, independent spending on behalf of favored candidates.

Involvement of groups concerned with tort law has been a longstanding feature of Ohio Supreme Court elections, but that involvement grew considerably between 1973 and 2012. The growth was primarily a result of the court's sharp movement toward pro-plaintiff policies in the early 1980s, movement that spurred the business community to engage in substantial efforts to reverse the trend. From that point on groups were the most important financiers of election campaigns, and they produced several exceptions to the traditional pattern of small-scale, low-visibility campaigns.

The business community played the key role in these developments. Its mobilization in the 1980s initiated a new era in supreme court campaigns. From then on, its financial contributions and independent spending were the primary force bringing about relatively high-visibility electoral contests, both directly and by motivating pro-plaintiff groups to engage in large-scale efforts of their own. Further, the efforts of business groups were the reason that most of the candidates they supported enjoyed funding advantages over their opponents.

For the most part, the activity of business groups was fairly predictable. Those groups were more likely to engage in large-scale efforts to influence election outcomes when the supreme court's tort policies had become unfavorable to their interests. Just as important, they were more likely to mobilize when the chances of securing a positive change in the court's policies through an election contest were relatively high: when a seat held by a pro-plaintiff justice was in play because that justice was vulnerable to defeat or, more often, was not running for reelection. If that seat was pivotal to the court's ideological balance, the incentive for business groups to intervene actively was even higher.

The heavy involvement of interest groups in elections to the Ohio Supreme Court might create a second mechanism for those elections to shape the court's policies. Anticipating the need to maintain group support or to avoid arousing group opposition in future elections, justices might modify their positions in tort law over time. We did not find evidence of such changes. This does not mean that state supreme court justices are immune to electoral pressures. In criminal justice in particular, there is significant evidence that the prospect of facing the voters does affect justices' choices (M. G. Hall 1987, 1992, 1995). But that does not appear to be the case with tort law in Ohio.

Ultimately, it was the voters who chose winners and losers in the contention over seats on the Ohio Supreme Court. The interest group activity that greatly increased the scale of campaign activity in some contests had one very clear effect: it motivated more voters to make choices in supreme court contests. In itself, however, that higher level of participation appears to have had little effect on election outcomes.

In contrast, the funding advantage enjoyed by most business-supported candidates *did* have an impact. Such an advantage is helpful in any election contest, no matter what the level of visibility is. Although it is impossible to specify the relationship between funding advantages and electoral outcomes, our analyses support the conclusion that the Ohio Supreme Court's decisive turn in a pro-defendant direction early in this century owed much to the advantage that the business community gave to most of the candidates it favored in open-seat contests.

Did voters act deliberately to achieve this result? If a yes or no answer is required, the answer has to be no. To start with, candidates for seats on the court and the groups that supported them generally gave voters little basis for attention to the consequences of elections for tort policy. True, torts did play a prominent part in the 2000 and 2002 campaigns, and it was the victories of Republican candidates in 2002 that first established what became a long-standing conservative majority on tort policy. And in many other elections, candidates and groups raised issues that were indirectly related to tort law, such as the business climate in the state or the quality of health care. But those messages were indirect, and in most contests they were not prominent. As a result, voters would have had trouble discerning that the outcome of a particular contest might determine which direction the supreme court would take in tort policy.

It is noteworthy that in some election years (e.g., 2006), voters overwhelmingly chose Democratic candidates for other statewide offices while still choosing Republicans for the supreme court, an odd result and possible evidence that voters did not understand the issues at stake in the judicial contests. More broadly, the advantages that caused Democrats to win some supreme court contests and Republicans to win others seemed to derive largely—perhaps primarily—from favorable name recognition. In turn, that name recognition was fostered by the spending of candidates and the independent groups that supported them. Thus, the increasingly consistent spending advantage of candidates supported by the business community may have had its greatest effects simply through making sure that voters knew those candidates.

The survey evidence on what voters knew also strongly suggests that they had only limited awareness of the policy stakes in supreme court contests even when the campaigns gave them the best opportunity to gain that awareness. Of course, it might be that even a small minority of voters who based their choices on tort issues were sufficient to swing election outcomes, but we did not find evidence for that possibility.

This is not to say that voters acted without any regard to policy. Despite the absence of supreme court candidates' party affiliations on the Ohio ballot, there is a substantial degree of party-line voting in elections to the court. Further, in the high-visibility contests that reflect primarily the activity of business groups, both voters' party identifications and their ideological leanings had a more powerful effect on their choices of candidates than they otherwise did. Even if voters did not have judicial policy firmly in mind, their collective decisions to elect a Democratic liberal or a Republican conservative (in those contests in which the competing candidates fit these descriptions) could be said to express a broader policy preference.

That said, in the story of membership and policy change told in this book, voters are best understood as secondary characters, swept along by events rather than actively shaping them. Of course, in this respect voters in Ohio Supreme Court elections are not very different from voters in elections to most other offices. Voters choose candidates for a variety of reasons, and in most election contests they have little information to work with. It is not surprising that in such contests they choose between candidates primarily on the basis of the kinds of information that are easiest to obtain, so that their collective decisions have effects on policy that they may not have anticipated or intended.

Understanding Judicial Elections

It has been three decades since legal scholar Roy Schotland reported that judicial elections "have now become noisier, nastier and costlier" (1985, 76). Since that time many other observers have reported a transformation in the scope and content of electoral campaigns for judgeships (e.g., Caufield 2007; Goldberg 2007; Sample et al. 2010; Gibson et al. 2011).

A transformation has indeed occurred. Acting on their perceptions of the high stakes involved in judicial elections, interest groups have increased their involvement in those elections. As a result, there has been a growth in contentious judicial races and in the number of races that are relatively visible to the voters (Hojnacki and Baum 1992b; Streb 2007; Sample et al. 2010).

But that transformation is limited and selective. For one thing, the developments on which observers focus are almost entirely at the supreme court level. Although elections at the trial and intermediate appellate levels receive little attention from scholars and reformers, what we know about them indicates that they have changed far less than supreme court elections.[1] That difference is understandable, indeed inevitable. The membership of state supreme courts has far greater impact on the policy goals of interest groups than does the composition of any specific lower courts. As a result, the very substantial growth in funding of campaigns found at the supreme court level has not occurred in intermediate appellate courts and trial courts (Streb and Frederick 2011).

Even at the supreme court level, interest groups focus on some states and some contests more than others. In Ohio, where groups concerned with tort law had good reason to make major commitments to judicial contests, the extent of those commitments has varied considerably across election years and specific contests. Moreover, supreme court contests that approach gubernatorial and senatorial elections in the level of campaign activity and visibility have been very much the exception to the rule. The same appears to be true of other states in which some supreme court elections are hotly contested (Sample et al. 2010).

Even so, the changes that have occurred in campaigns for positions on state supreme courts are consequential. What has happened in Ohio underlines the significance of those changes. At the same time, the extent of those changes should not be exaggerated even when and where the changes have been most pronounced.

Spending by candidates, parties, and supportive groups has raised the profile of many supreme court contests. Of course, that is not the goal of these individuals and organizations; rather, they want to win elections in order to shape judicial policy. The business community and other interest groups that care about tort cases seek to staff supreme courts with justices who share their positions on personal injury law.

This does not mean that interest groups and the candidates they support necessarily campaign on the basis of the issues they care about. Rather, they seek the most effective ways to appeal to voters, whatever those ways may be. Sometimes they do give some emphasis to the economic issues that motivate them. In the decisive 2002 Ohio elections, as we have noted, torts played a prominent role in the campaigns.

On the whole, however, candidates and groups emphasize criminal justice issues. Because criminal justice is a valence issue, with the great majority of voters favoring pro-prosecution policies, depicting a candidate as soft on crime can be an effective tactic. Largely as a result, criminal justice has become a recurrent theme of television commercials in supreme court contests (Greytak et al. 2015, 48–65). The defeats of three California justices in the 1986 retention elections—elections that were the most prominent harbinger of change in state supreme court elections—were based on the effectiveness of an opposition campaign that emphasized criminal justice in general and the death penalty in particular. Behind the scenes, however, the California campaign was largely financed by groups with an interest in economic issues (Wold and Culver 1987, 350; Reidinger 1987, 58).

Criminal justice issues have not played a significant part in contests for the Ohio Supreme Court, perhaps because sitting justices have been careful to avoid making themselves vulnerable to charges of softness on crime.[2] In two highly visible contests, the 1984 and 1986 campaigns involving the Celebrezze brothers, groups that sought the defeat of those incumbents emphasized questions about their fitness for office. Aided by supportive newspapers, they made that issue the centerpiece of the contests. More often, as we have noted, groups' primary goal has been to establish positive name recognition for the candidates they favored. The same appears to be true in most other states in which economic groups have participated actively in supreme court contests through monetary contributions and independent spending.

Increasingly, research on supreme court elections has moved beyond campaigns to consider the role of voters (e.g., Bonneau and Cann 2015; M. G. Hall 2015). Even so, we know little about the connections between campaign activity and the bases for voters' decisions. Our inquiry into those connections in Ohio suggests that the economic issues underlying changes in supreme court contests play an even more limited role in voters' choices between candidates than they do in campaigns by and for the candidates. Rather, voters act primarily on information that is more readily available to them and easier to assimilate.

The same is probably true in other states. When policy-related matters make a decisive difference in supreme court elections, they tend to involve criminal justice, a more vivid issue than economic issues such as torts and one on which public opinion is strongly on one side. Frequently, and probably most of the time, voters respond not to policy issues of any type but rather to other types of information. Heated electoral battles between pro-plaintiff and pro-defendant groups in Alabama and Texas produced distinctly more pro-defendant courts (Ware 1999; Cheek and Champagne 2005). But it seems likely that the combination of a pro-Republican realignment of voters and a partisan judicial ballot, not voters' preferences on tort policy, was the primary source of the outcomes in those two states.

Despite the burgeoning of research on supreme court elections, there is still a need for additional research to provide a fuller picture of those elections. This is especially true of voting behavior, and there is a particular need for better understanding of the linkages between campaign activity and voters' choices. More extensive evidence of those linkages will provide us with a clearer picture of the functioning of judicial elections, and it will also facilitate evaluation of elections as a means to select supreme court justices.

Evaluating Judicial Elections

Our reference to evaluation of elections is a reminder of the normative issues that arise from the practice of electing judges. Debates over alternative methods for selecting judges are a permanent feature of American politics, and questions about the desirability of judicial elections have been central to those debates for more than a century (Dubois 1980, chap. 1; Shugerman 2012). Growth in the incidence of high-visibility contests for supreme court seats and a perception of fundamental changes in the scope and content of campaigns for those seats have heated up the disagreement over judicial elections.

The issues involved in the contention over judicial elections range widely. Our inquiry in this book allows us to offer thoughts about some of those issues, especially concerns that have been expressed about "politicization" of the courts through elections.

One element of politicization is the role of interest groups in judicial campaigns. Recognizing the importance of the state courts in influencing policy, interest groups have ratcheted up their attacks on judicial candidates, especially incumbent justices, and they are more likely to raise issues involving judicial policy (Goldberg 2007; Sample et al. 2010). The growth in television advertising has enabled interest groups to broadcast attacks on opponents and issue positions more widely to voters.

Contests for the Ohio Supreme Court have included the kinds of campaign tactics by outside interests that judicial reform groups, such as Justice at Stake, find objectionable. The television advertising in 2000 that depicted Justice Alice Robie Resnick as corrupt was widely decried, and one of the ads was eventually judged by the Ohio Elections Commission to have a false statement about Resnick's record on the court (Nash 2005). Some candidates have explicitly allied themselves with the agendas of political parties or interest groups, and issue-oriented advertising has been common. There was also the highly unusual effort by Chief Justice Frank Celebrezze in 1984 to boost the reelection prospects of his brother James through refunds of public utility charges to Ohio consumers. Chief Justice Celebrezze was the target of very strong attacks during his own reelection campaign in 1986.

In considering the series of electoral contests that ultimately transformed the Ohio Supreme Court, evaluation of their content depends largely on attitudes toward issue-oriented campaigning. Many of those contests featured substantial amounts of advertising that referred directly or indirectly to judicial issues. But if one thinks that such advertising is acceptable, overall the content of campaigns was not especially objectionable. A great deal of what candidates and their supporters did took the traditional approach of seeking to develop positive name recognition with themes that had little to do with judicial issues.

Some of the attacks on incumbents were strong—the allegations in 1986 that Chief Justice Celebrezze had mob connections, the anti-Resnick commercials in 2000. But Ohio has generally not featured the most outrageous campaign tactics in the country. In contrast with other states, no Ohio Supreme Court candidate has been depicted as a skunk by his opponents, no candidate who sits on a court with only civil jurisdiction has been criticized for never handing down a death sentence, and no candidate in a party primary has brought ethics charges against three opponents and then attacked them for being the targets of ethics investigations (M. G. Hall 2015, 71).

It may be problematic, however, that campaign contributions and independent spending in large amounts were used to transform the Ohio court's tort policies largely sub rosa: business groups sought tort policies that were favorable to defendants without usually presenting their true intentions to voters. Instead, to the extent that campaigns were about issues at all, their messages were often couched in broader terms about concern over judicial activism or the ideological leaning of the court. Such objections would apply to other states as well, especially those in which attacks on incumbent justices were framed in terms of social issues but the goal underlying those attacks was to gain a more business-friendly court.

Of course, ideological transformation of courts through membership change occurs in appointive systems as well as in states that elect judges. The impact of presidential appointments on the US Supreme Court is familiar to observers of the Court, and increasingly presidents have sought to achieve similar impact on the courts of appeals. At the state level, governors often use their appointment powers for the same ideological purposes as presidents.[3] As they do in elections, interest groups attempt to influence judicial appointments (Caldeira and Wright 1995; Steigerwalt 2010), and they are not always wholly frank with the public about their reasons.

Still, transformation of supreme courts by presidents and governors is arguably less problematic than similar transformation through judicial elections. Voters who choose chief executives have a good opportunity to recognize the potential impact of their choices on a broad range of policies that includes the selection of judges. Whether or not Supreme Court appointments are a prominent issue in presidential campaigns, any reasonably alert voter understands that the outcome of an election could have a substantial effect on the Court. In the 2016 presidential election, the importance of the outcome for the makeup of the Court was almost impossible to miss given the controversy over President Obama's opportunity to nominate a successor to the Court after Justice Antonin Scalia's death and the Republican-controlled Senate's refusal to provide a hearing to the president's nominee, Merrick Garland.

A considerably higher level of alertness may be required for voters in state supreme court elections to recognize the potential effect of their choices. Election of judges provides a mechanism for direct popular control over the courts that is understandably attractive to those who support accountability of judges to the public (see Bonneau and Hall 2009). But with the exception of issues that are highly publicized in campaigns, as criminal justice sometimes is, conscious public influence over the courts' policy outputs may be more likely when judges are appointed than when they are chosen directly by the public.

In reality, states that allow for election of judges are unlikely to give up that system. If that is true, then we might want to encourage judicial candidates to make their policy positions explicit rather than discouraging them from doing so. Certainly there could be concerns about further politicizing the courts and undermining their legitimacy if judicial candidates acted more like politicians, although studies find that the perceived negative consequences of this increasing politicization are exaggerated (Bonneau, Hall, and Streb 2011; Gibson 2012; M. G. Hall 2015), and candidates, especially incumbents, may continue to be reluctant to state their policy positions directly. Nevertheless, if the outcome of a supreme court contest is likely to determine the court's direction in tort law, it would seem better for voters to understand the stakes in the outcome. For the same reason, the news media and organizations that seek to inform the voters arguably should publicize those stakes. However, both may be strongly inclined not to do so. In the case of "good government" groups, that inclination derives from a view that such information should be irrelevant to voters' choices.

Another possible step is to indicate the candidates' political party affiliations on the ballot. The movement away from partisan judicial elections and toward nonpartisan elections in the late nineteenth century and the early twentieth century has had long-lasting effects: of the states that have "regular" elections of judges (as distinguished from retention elections), two-thirds use a nonpartisan ballot. Along with Arizona and Michigan, Ohio has a hybrid system in which judges are nominated on a partisan basis but the general election ballot is nonpartisan.

The nonpartisan ballot has hardly kept Ohio's political parties out of the election process. Party organizations play an active role in selecting prospective nominees for judgeships, and they are also active in the funding of campaigns. By distributing sample ballots, they alert some voters to the party affiliations of judicial candidates. But most voters cast their ballots for judges with no certainty about what those affiliations are.

For many observers of judicial elections (e.g., Corriher 2012; see Champagne 2001b), that lack of knowledge is a good thing because party affiliations should be irrelevant to the selection of judges. However, there are strong arguments to be made for more widespread knowledge of party affiliations. State supreme courts make important policy choices, and those choices correlate with justices' party affiliations. When voters know what those affiliations are, they are in a better position to shape the direction of judicial policy in ways that accord with their own views and interests.

Of course, the correlation between party affiliations and policy positions is imperfect. In Ohio, the pro-plaintiff positions of Republicans Andrew Douglas and Paul Pfeifer in tort law produced a long delay in the development of a stable conservative majority on the court. But on the whole, Democratic and Republican justices differ in their positions on economic issues in the direction that would be expected. When Ohio voters made the collective choices between 2002 and 2006 that produced a strongly pro-business court, the candidates' party affiliations were an accurate guide to their positions. This does not mean that with a partisan ballot Ohio voters would have known that their choices would determine the general direction of the supreme court's policies in tort law or even that tort law was an important issue in the supreme court. But most voters would at least have had reason to think that their choices would help determine the court's ideological direction, just as presidential voters do for the US Supreme Court.

Certainly there is room for disagreement about the best way to choose state judges. In making judgments about that issue, however, it is important to keep in mind the differences between supreme courts and lower courts. For one thing, as we have noted, the changes in the character of judicial elections that scholars and other observers have emphasized are largely limited to the supreme court level. For those who see these changes as undesirable, changes in selection systems to remedy them do not necessarily need to be applied to other courts. If it is accurate to characterize changes in supreme court elections over the past several decades as a process of politicization, that politicization has not extended much beyond the states' highest courts.

Just as important, state supreme courts play a role in the making of public policy that differs from the roles of lower courts. Supreme courts do not necessarily have a greater impact than the courts below them: in criminal law or tort law, to take two examples, decisions by judges and juries in individual cases affect a great many people directly. But supreme courts establish legal rules that apply statewide, shaping policy in broad terms. The importance of those legal rules gives interest groups a strong incentive to participate in supreme court elections, an incentive that is far weaker in elections to lower courts. By the same token, voters' choices in individual contests for supreme courts are far more consequential than their choices in individual contests for trial courts and courts of appeals. In thinking about how best to select judges, it seems wise to take that difference into account.

As this discussion indicates, judgments about how judges should be selected depend largely on normative premises. People who begin with different premises may draw very different implications from the same empirical picture. Those who believe that judicial elections are needed because they allow the public to hold judges accountable will likely view what happened in Ohio fairly positively. Judges who contributed to major policy changes were not able to do so with impunity; they had to face voters in elections every six years, interest groups concerned about the court's direction were sometimes able to focus considerable attention on the court and individual judges, and occasionally incumbents lost their bids for reelection. Those who are concerned about the politicization of judicial politics no doubt see the findings differently. In their eyes, business groups purposely politicized the process, and voters were duped into supporting the business-backed candidates. Elections did not promote accountability but instead potentially undermined the public's view of the court because of the character of the campaigns.

We do not take a side in that long-argued debate. But we strongly believe that, regardless of their normative premises, those who participate in the discussions over selection systems should fully take into account the empirical picture generated by a robust literature on the process of electing judges and its causes and consequences. As we hope we have demonstrated in this book, to truly grasp what is contained in that picture requires careful attention to group activity, voter behavior, the legal policy courts produce, and the complex ways in which all of these interact.

APPENDIX 1

Cast of Characters

To assist readers in following the discussions of supreme court elections and policies discussed in the text, we provide some information that can be used as a point of reference. The first list includes justices who served for at least two years in the period from 1981 through 2014. The justices' tenure on the court and their party affiliation are given in parentheses. The second list includes the interest groups that were substantially involved in judicial contests.

Justices

CLIFFORD BROWN (D, 1981–86). Although Clifford Brown served only one term on the court, he was an important participant in the court's pro-plaintiff innovations in tort law during the early 1980s.

HERBERT BROWN (D, 1987–92). During his single term on the court, Herbert Brown took a moderate position in tort law. As a result, his replacement by Republican Paul Pfeifer in 1992 actually made the court more liberal.

WILLIAM BROWN (D, 1973–84). William Brown took a relatively conservative position for a Democrat in tort law and thus did not contribute substantially to the liberal innovations of the early 1980s.

YVETTE MCGEE BROWN (D, 2011–12). Appointed by the Democratic governor in 2011, Yvette McGee Brown was the sole Democrat on the court and appeared to be close with Republican chief justice Maureen O'Connor. Even with her business background and her ability to get along well with her Republican colleagues, she lost her election for a full term in 2012.

FRANK CELEBREZZE (D, 1972–86). Elected as an associate justice in 1972 and as chief justice in 1978, in the early 1980s Frank Celebrezze led and symbolized major doctrinal changes that favored tort plaintiffs. He became the subject of controversy for his leadership of the court. He was defeated for reelection in 1986 by Thomas Moyer in a contentious, high-profile campaign that centered on criticism of Celebrezze but that was motivated in part by the court's policies.

JAMES CELEBREZZE (D, 1983–84). Brother of Chief Justice Frank Celebrezze, James Celebrezze defeated appointed incumbent Blanche Krupansky for a seat as associate justice in 1982. Two years later he was defeated for a full term by J. Craig Wright in a heated and well-publicized campaign.

DEBORAH COOK (R, 1995–2003). Cook took a conservative position in tort law. Her reelection campaign against Tim Black in 2000 was overshadowed by the contest between Alice Robie Resnick and Terrence O'Donnell, but it still received considerable attention.

ROBERT CUPP (R, 2007–12). Cupp's election in 2006 created an all-Republican court and reinforced the court's conservatism in tort law. He lost to William O'Neill in 2012 despite outspending O'Neill $750,000 to $5,000, a loss that probably resulted primarily from the power of Irish names in elections to the Ohio Supreme Court.

ANDREW (ANDY) DOUGLAS (R, 1985–2002). Douglas's election in 1984 helped reduce the Democratic majority on the court. But he had ties to the labor movement, and as an associate justice he took liberal positions on tort issues. His 2002 retirement, required by state age rules, led to the election of Republican Maureen O'Connor, which established a conservative majority in tort law.

JUDITH (JUDI) FRENCH (R, 2013–PRESENT). French was elected to succeed fellow Republican Evelyn Stratton.

ROBERT HOLMES (R, 1978–92). Holmes took a pro-defendant position in opposition to the court's liberal direction in the early 1980s and in accord with the partial reversal of that direction later on.

JUDITH LANZINGER (R, 2005–16). Lanzinger was elected to the court in 2004, succeeding the retiring Democrat Francis Sweeney. Her replacement of a pro-plaintiff justice solidified the pro-defendant majority on the court, and that potential change resulted in a relatively well-funded campaign on her behalf.

RALPH S. LOCHER (D, 1977–88). Locher was one of two Democrats elected in 1976 to give the party a majority on the court. Because he leaned in a pro-defendant direction, he did not contribute to the court's growing liberalism in tort policy in the early 1980s.

THOMAS MOYER (R, 1987–2010). Moyer's defeat of Frank Celebrezze for chief justice in a high-profile 1986 contest gave the court a Republican majority that has continued since that time. Moyer served as chief justice for two dozen years, taking a position in tort law that was conservative but less pro-defendant than that of some Republican colleagues.

MAUREEN O'CONNOR (R, 2003–PRESENT). As lieutenant governor of Ohio, O'Connor was elected associate justice in 2002 in a high-profile contest and was elected chief justice in 2010. When she succeeded pro-plaintiff Republican Andrew Douglas on the court, the court gained a pro-defendant majority that it has maintained since that time.

TERRENCE O'DONNELL (R, 2003–PRESENT). As the challenger to Alice Robie Resnick in 2000, O'Donnell benefited from large-scale spending by business groups but lost the contest. His appointment to the court in 2003 and subsequent election in 2004 maintained the court's conservative majority.

WILLIAM O'NEILL (D, 2013–PRESENT). Not to be confused with former chief justice C. William O'Neill, this O'Neill was elected to the court in 2012 after two previous failed attempts. He refused to take campaign contributions because of the influence he believed money has on justices.

PAUL PFEIFER (R, 1993–2016). A longtime state legislator, Pfeifer was elected to the court in 1992. A Republican, he was also a former trial lawyer, and he took a strong pro-plaintiff position in tort cases. He was reelected three times, the last two times without opposition. His presence alongside Andrew Douglas between 1993 and 2002 meant that the court had both a Republican majority and a pro-plaintiff majority.

ALICE ROBIE RESNICK (D, 1988–2006). After winning two elections to the court, in 2000 Resnick faced a strong election challenge from business groups that charged her with favoring pro-plaintiff groups that had funded her campaigns with favorable rulings. After a large-scale campaign with heavy spending on both sides, she was reelected.

EVELYN LUNDBERG STRATTON (R, 1996–2012). Stratton was nicknamed the "Velvet Hammer" for her criminal justice policies. First appointed and then elected to the court in 1996, she faced challenger Janet Burnside in 2002. Because ideological control of the court was at stake, the two candidates were very well funded and benefited from high levels of independent spending. Stratton's victory, combined with the election of Maureen O'Connor, created what became a long-standing conservative majority on tort issues.

A. WILLIAM SWEENEY (D, 1977–94). During his long tenure on the court, Sweeney was one of the leaders in the court's liberal innovations in tort law in the early 1980s and maintained a pro-plaintiff position in the field.

FRANCIS E. SWEENEY (D, 1993–2004). Even more than A. William Sweeney, Francis Sweeney had a strongly pro-plaintiff voting record in tort cases.

J. CRAIG WRIGHT (R, 1985–96). Wright defeated James Celebrezze in 1984 in the first of the high-profile supreme court contests of the current era. Unlike Andrew Douglas, another Republican elected in 1984, Wright took a pro-defendant stance in tort law. There was a scuffle between Wright and Douglas in 1991, apparently precipitated by an unfavorable news story about Wright.

Interest Groups

BUSINESS GROUPS. Groups in the business community have been the primary source of support for pro-defendant candidates for the Ohio Supreme Court. Because of their high stakes in tort cases, insurance groups have been among the most important participants in supreme court contests. As a representative of the business community, the Ohio Chamber of Commerce has participated actively in contests for the court through funding of candidates' campaigns and independent spending. Citizens for a Strong Ohio, organized by the Chamber, carried out a large-scale independent campaign against Alice Robie Resnick in 2000.

LABOR UNIONS. The AFL-CIO and individual unions have long been an important source of endorsements and funding support for supreme court candidates with liberal positions on economic issues, including torts. While generally supporting Democratic candidates, labor groups have supported pro-plaintiff Republicans as well.

MEDICAL COMMUNITY. Because of their concern about medical malpractice suits, groups in the health care industry have made financial contributions to supreme court candidates who took pro-defendant positions. These groups have been especially active since 2002, and in 2002 spending by medical groups and personal involvement by physicians were important to the successful campaigns of Republican candidates that created a pro-defendant majority on the court.

TRIAL LAWYERS. This is a common term for attorneys who represent plaintiffs (primarily individuals) in lawsuits for monetary damages and, more specifically, in the tort cases that constitute a high proportion of all civil damages suits. Through organizations such as the Ohio Academy of Trial Lawyers (now the Ohio Association for Justice), trial lawyers have provided a substantial share of campaign funding for supreme court candidates whom they perceive as pro-plaintiff.

APPENDIX 2

Outcomes of Ohio Supreme Court Elections, 1976–2016

YEAR	FOR CHIEF JUSTICE	DEMOCRAT	REPUBLICAN	INDEPENDENT
1976		**A. William Sweeney**	Don P. Brown	
		Ralph S. Locher	William J. Morrissey	
1978	**x**	**Frank D. Celebrezze (i)**	Thomas M. Herbert (i)	
		William B. Brown (I)	Richard M. Markus	
		Clifford F. Brown	**Paul W. Brown (I)**	
1980	**x**	**Frank D. Celebrezze (I)**	Sara J. Harper	
		Lawrence Grey	Robert E. Holmes (a)	
		Clifford F. Brown	David D. Dowd Jr. (a)	
1982		**A. William Sweeney (I)**	John W. McCormac	
		Ralph S. Locher (I)	William J. McCrone	
		James D. Celebrezze	Blanche Krupansky (a)	
1984		John E. Corrigan	**Andrew Douglas**	
		James P. Celebrezze (I)	**Craig Wright**	
1986	x	Frank D. Celebrezze (I)	**Thomas J. Moyer**	
		Francis E. Sweeney	**Robert E. Holmes (I)**	
		Herbert R. Brown	Joyce J. George	
1988		**A. William Sweeney (I)**	Paul R. Matia	
		Alice Robie Resnick	Joyce J. George	
1990		Stuart J. Banks	**Andrew Douglas (I)**	
		Stephanie Tubbs Jones	**Craig Wright (I)**	J. Ross Haffey
1992	x	Robert H. Gorman	**Thomas J. Moyer (I)**	J. Ross Haffey
		Francis E. Sweeney	Mark R. Painter	
		John T. Patton	**Paul E. Pfeifer**	
1994		J. Ross Haffey	**Deborah Cook**	
		Alice Robie Resnick (I)	Sara J. Harper	

(continued)

YEAR	FOR CHIEF JUSTICE	DEMOCRAT	REPUBLICAN	INDEPENDENT
1996		Peter M. Sikora	**Andrew Douglas (I)**	
		Marianna Brown Bettman	**Evelyn L. Stratton (a)**	
1998	x	Gary Tyack	**Thomas J. Moyer (I)**	
		Francis E. Sweeney (I)	Stephen W. Powell	
		Ronald Suster	**Paul E. Pfeifer (I)**	
2000		Tim Black	**Deborah Cook (I)**	
		Alice Robie Resnick (I)	Terrence O'Donnell	
2002		Tim Black	**Maureen O'Connor**	
		Janet Burnside	**Evelyn L. Stratton (I)**	
2004	x	C. Ellen Connally	**Thomas J. Moyer (I)**	
		William M. O'Neill	**Terrence O'Donnell (a)**	
		Nancy A. Fuerst	**Judith Ann Lanzinger**	
		(no candidate)	**Paul E. Pfeifer (I)**	
2006		William M. O'Neill	**Terrence O'Donnell (I)**	
		Ben Espy	**Robert R. Cupp**	
2008		Joseph Russo	**Maureen O'Connor (I)**	
		Peter M. Sikora	**Evelyn L. Stratton (I)**	
2010	x	Eric Brown (a)	**Maureen O'Connor (i)**	
		Mary Jane Trapp	**Judith Ann Lanzinger (I)**	
		(no candidate)	**Paul E. Pfeifer (I)**	
2012		Michael Skindell	**Terrence O'Donnell (I)**	
		William M. O'Neill	Robert R. Cupp (I)	
		Yvette McGee Brown (a)	**Sharon Kennedy**	
2014		Tom Letson	**Sharon Kennedy (I)**	
		John P. O'Donnell	**Judi French (a)**	
2016	x	(no candidate)	**Maureen O'Connor (I)**	
		John P. O'Donnell	**Pat Fischer**	
		Cynthia Rice	**Pat DeWine**	

Boldface indicates the winning candidate.
a An appointee who had not yet won an election
I Incumbent who had won a previous election
i Incumbent associate justice running for election as chief justice

APPENDIX 3

Partisan Makeup of the Ohio Supreme Court, 1977–2017

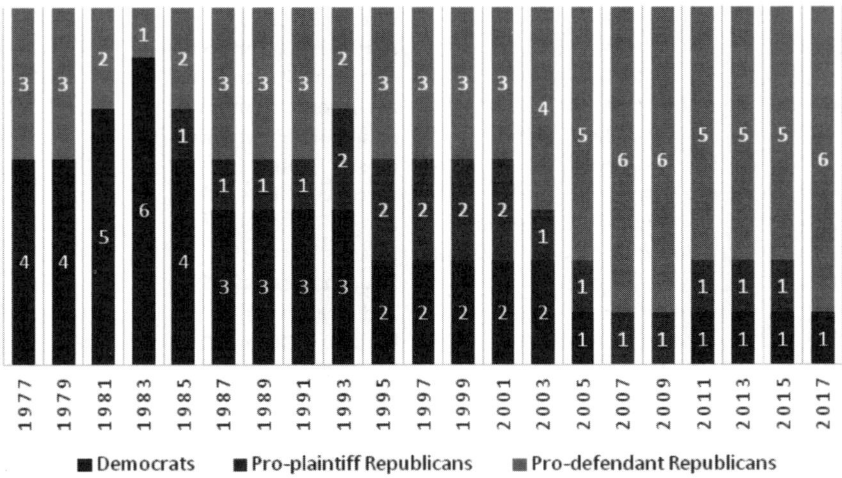

Note: Where the partisan makeup of the court changed during a biennium, the chart shows the membership as of the beginning of the biennium. The pro-plaintiff Republicans are Andrew Douglas and Paul E. Pfeifer.

NOTES

INTRODUCTION

1. In Illinois, as in some other states, supreme court justices are elected from districts rather than from the state as a whole.
2. The actual amount that State Farm contributed is disputed. Karmeier's campaign stated that they received $350,000 from State Farm. However, the plaintiffs in the State Farm case allege that the insurance company actually gave anywhere from $2.4 to $4 million to the campaign by funneling money through the Illinois Chamber of Commerce and the Illinois Civil Justice League, a tort reform group. "Justice for the Highest Bidder?" *Chicago Tribune,* November 21, 2011.
3. All of the quotations in the next few paragraphs were taken directly from television advertisements in the Karmeier/Maag race. To view those commercials, visit http://www.brennancenter.org/analysis/buying-time-2004-illinois (accessed July 15, 2014).
4. Avery v. State Farm Mutual Automobile Insurance Company, 216 Ill. 2d 100 (2005). One of the court's seven justices did not participate in the case.
5. Major studies of these phenomena include Bonneau and Hall (2009), Gibson (2012), Bonneau and Cann (2015), M. G. Hall (2015), and Kritzer (2015).
6. The scholarship on elections and judicial behavior is summarized and discussed in Kritzer (2015, 59–76). The impact of interest group campaigns on economic policies in state supreme courts has been examined in studies of Alabama (Ware 1999) and Texas (Cheek and Champagne 2005).
7. The history of judicial selection systems in the United States is discussed in Berkson (1980), Hanssen (2004), and Shugerman (2012). We draw our account largely from Shugerman.
8. This is a good place to discuss terminology relating to the two competing sides in Ohio Supreme Court elections. We refer to the side that favors the positions of defendants in tort law primarily as "business" or "the business community." This is because the interests of the business community generally match those of tort defendants, whether because the defendant is itself a business or because an insur-

ance company will ultimately bear the costs if the defendant loses. These labels encompass medical professionals and institutions that are not businesses as such but that sometimes ally themselves with business in supreme court elections and other arenas. The other side, on which the major participants in Ohio have been labor unions and trial lawyers who represent tort plaintiffs, we generally label as "pro-plaintiff," except when we refer to specific groups within the pro-plaintiff coalition. When referring to supreme court candidates and justices, we use the label "pro-plaintiff" for those who tend to vote for, or are expected to vote for, plaintiffs in tort cases and either "pro-defendant" or "pro-business" for those who favor, or are expected to favor, the other side.

9. The report simply documented an increase in spending in judicial elections. It provided no evidence that perceptions of the courts were indeed changing.
10. Republican Party v. White, 536 U.S. 765, 782 (2002).
11. Ibid., 788.
12. Commentators sometimes refer to change in judicial campaigns generally, not just campaigns at the supreme court level. But supreme courts have been the focus of both commentary and empirical research. What we do know about campaigns for seats on lower courts suggests that those campaigns have not changed nearly to the same degree, if indeed they have changed at all (see Frederick and Streb 2008; Streb, Frederick, LaFrance, and Rice 2017).
13. These figures include states with retention elections as well as those with elections contested by candidates, but spending in judicial retention elections is generally low compared with candidate elections.
14. This body of research is summarized and analyzed in Kritzer (2015, chap. 3).
15. In addition to the scholarly research on campaign contributions and decisional behavior, there have also been news articles about the relationship between the two, including a long 2006 article in the *New York Times* that focused on the Ohio Supreme Court (Liptak and Roberts 2006).
16. The two largest Arizona counties use nominating commissions and retention elections to select their trial judges. In Michigan, incumbent justices are automatically placed on the ballot. Information on selection methods is from "Judicial Selection in the States" on the website maintained by the National Center for State Courts (http://www.judicialselection.us/).
17. The history of judicial selection in Ohio is described in Solimine and Saphire (2004).
18. Ballot measures to adopt the Missouri Plan were defeated by 2-1 margins in 1938 and 1987 (Barkdull 1939; Felice and Kilwein 1992). Had voters approved the 1938 proposal, the system it created presumably would be called the Ohio Plan; Missouri did not adopt this system until 1940. The decisions on the federal lawsuit were Ohio Council 8 American Federation of State, County, and Municipal Employees v. Brunner, 24 F. Supp. 3d 680 (S.D. Ohio 2014); and Ohio Council 8 American Federation of State, County, and Municipal Employees v. Husted, 814 F.3d 329 (6th Cir. 2016).
19. Streb (2007) found considerable involvement by party organizations in trial court elections in states with nonpartisan systems, and the degree of involvement almost surely is much higher in supreme court elections.

20. For a discussion of the difficulties of classifying Ohio (and Michigan) as partisan or nonpartisan, see Nelson, Caufield, and Martin (2013).

ONE The Course of Tort Policy

1. Primes v. Tyler, 43 Ohio St. 2d 195 (1975).
2. Varholla v. Varholla, 56 Ohio St. 2d 269 (1978); Keaton v. Ribbeck, 58 Ohio St. 2d 443 (1979); and Thrash v. Hill, 63 Ohio St. 2d 178 (1980), respectively.
3. Avellone v. St. John's Hospital, 165 Ohio St. 467 (1956).
4. Albritton v. Neighborhood Centers Association for Child Development, 12 Ohio St. 3d 210 (1984).
5. Bonkowsky v. Bonkowsky, 69 Ohio St. 2d 152 (1982); and Karam v. Allstate Insurance Co., 70 Ohio St. 2d 227 (1982).
6. Prem v. Cox, 2 Ohio St. 3d 149 (1983).
7. Dorsey v. State Farm Mutual Automobile Insurance Co., 9 Ohio St. 3d 27 (1984).
8. Kirchner v. Crystal, 15 Ohio St. 3d 326 (1984); and Shearer v. Shearer, 18 Ohio St. 3d 94 (1985).
9. Sears v. City of Cincinnati, 31 Ohio St. 2d 157, 161 (1972).
10. Thacker v. Board of Trustees, 35 Ohio St. 2d 49 (1973).
11. Schenkolewski v. Cleveland Metroparks System, 67 Ohio St. 2d 31, 36 (1981); for boards of education, Carbone v. Overfield, 6 Ohio St. 3d 212 (1983); for park districts, Marrek v. Cleveland Metroparks Board of Commissioners, 9 Ohio St. 3d 194; for public libraries, Mathis v. Cleveland Public Library, 9 Ohio St. 3d 199; and for municipalities, Enghauser Manufacturing Co. v. Eriksson Engineering Ltd., 6 Ohio St. 3d 31, 35 (1983).
12. Elston v. Howland Local Schools, 113 Ohio St. 3d 314, 323 (2007).
13. Ohio Code § 2744.03.
14. State ex rel. Munding v. Industrial Commission of Ohio, 92 Ohio St. 434 (1915).
15. Quoted in Blankenship v. Cincinnati Milacron Chemicals, Inc., 69 Ohio St. 2d 608, 612 (1982).
16. *Blankenship,* 69 Ohio St. 2d 608.
17. Jones v. VIP Development Co., 15 Ohio St. 3d 90 (1984).
18. Mitchell v. Lawson Milk Co., Ohio St. 3d 190, 193 (1988).
19. Brady v. Safety-Kleen Corporation, 61 Ohio St. 3d 624 (1991).
20. Johnson v. BP Chemicals, Inc., 85 Ohio St. 3d 298 (1999).
21. *Johnson,* 85 Ohio St. 3d 298, 304.
22. Kaminski v. Metal & Wire Products Co., 125 Ohio St. 3d 250 (2010); Houdek v. Thyssenkrupp Materials N.A., Inc., 134 Ohio St. 3d 491 (2012).
23. The court's decisions were DeRolph v. State, 78 Ohio St. 3d 193 (1997), 89 Ohio St. 3d 1(2000), 93 Ohio St. 3d 309 (2001), and 97 Ohio St. 3d 434 (2002), and State ex rel. State of Ohio v. Lewis, 99 Ohio St. 3d 97 (2003).
24. A statute of limitations sets a deadline for the filing of a legal action, based on when an injury occurred; a statute of repose sets a deadline based on when the defendant took an action that resulted in an injury.
25. State ex rel. Ohio Academy of Trial Lawyers v. Sheward, 86 Ohio St. 3d 451, fn. 6 (1999).
26. The court also held that the law violated the Ohio Constitution's one-subject rule.

27. Arbino v. Johnson & Johnson, 116 Ohio St. 3d 468 (2007).
28. Groch v. General Motors Corp., 117 Ohio St. 3d 192 (2008); and Ruther v. Kaiser, 134 Ohio St. 3d 408 (2012).
29. Opinions aside, in 1991 Craig Wright (of the pro-defendant camp) and Andrew Douglas (of the pro-plaintiff camp) got into an argument in another justice's office that culminated in a brief physical battle that left Douglas with broken ribs. However, this conflict did not appear to relate to their disagreements over policy (Yost 1991b).
30. Paugh v. Hanks, 6 Ohio St. 3d 72, 74 (1983).
31. *Blankenship,* 69 Ohio St. 2d 608, 616. This opinion was joined by A. William Sweeney and Clifford Brown.
32. Shroades v. Rental Homes, Inc., 68 Ohio St. 2d 20, 29 (1981).
33. Hutchinson v. J. C. Penney Casualty Insurance Co., 17 Ohio St. 3d 195, 203 (1985).
34. *Arbino,* 116 Ohio St. 3d 468, 518–19.
35. Schaefer v. Allstate Insurance Co., 76 Ohio St. 3d 553, 558–60 (1996, citations omitted).
36. We began with this search in Lexis: COURT(supreme) and (tort or injur! or insurance or damages or negligence or liability or immunity) and NOT NAME(tax or parole or bar as! or "State of Ohio" or "Disciplinary Counsel" or "Industrial Commission") and NOT "decision without published opinion." We then removed cases that did not fit the criteria for inclusion.
37. In this analysis and the regression that follows, we omit the small number of cases with mixed outcomes.
38. These estimates were obtained using the Clarify program in Stata (Tomz, Wittenberg, and King 2003).
39. Justice Douglas was widely known as Andy, but we use his formal name in the book.
40. Like Sweeney, Douglas began with a moderate voting record before moving far to the pro-plaintiff side, and so there is a marked difference between long-term and short-term effects in the shift from William Brown to Douglas.
41. The number of other justices who participate in a case is frequently less than six because justices recuse themselves or are unavailable for other reasons. Ordinarily, justices who are absent from a case are replaced with visiting judges from the courts of appeals. We did not take those judges into account in our calculations.
42. Because our analysis of votes began in 1973, we omit any tort cases in which Celebrezze participated in late 1972, just after he joined the court.
43. The figure 328 times is as of October 2015; Westfield Insurance Co. v. Galatis, 100 Ohio St. 3d 216 (2003).
44. Scott-Pontzer v. Liberty Mut. Fire Ins. Co., 85 Ohio St.3d 660 (1999).
45. One study found evidence that campaign contributions had more limited effects on votes in economic cases for justices who could not run for reelection because of mandatory retirement ages (Shepherd 2009, 672–74). The difference between that finding and ours may reflect the effectiveness of Ohio interest groups in identifying supreme court candidates whose personal views align with group interests. The evidence on the effects of impending retirement on responsiveness to voters in capital punishment cases is mixed (Brace and Boyea 2007; Canes-Wrone, Clark, and Kelly 2014).

TWO Campaigns and Elections

1. Political parties certainly have an interest in shaping the makeup of the court. However, our focus is mostly on interest groups because party activity is often driven by interest group activity. Interest groups tend to be significant contributors to parties, who, in turn, use that money on behalf of judicial candidates.
2. Because of data limitations, the starting point is different for each figure. Figure 2.1 shows coverage only from the *Columbus Dispatch*. We also analyzed the content in the *Cleveland Plain Dealer*, but only had a comprehensive set of articles starting in 1992. As a result, we decided to include coverage from the *Dispatch* alone because it covered more years. We did note that the amount of coverage for each race for which we had comprehensive coverage was consistent between the two newspapers (Pearson's correlation = .83).
3. See "Cash v. Quality," *Cleveland Plain Dealer,* March 5, 2008, B8.
4. Gubernatorial appointment of justices to the Ohio Supreme Court is the exception to the rule. But it has happened several times, including most recently in 2011 when Democratic governor Ted Strickland appointed Yvette McGee Brown to replace Maureen O'Connor (who left her seat as associate justice when she was elected chief justice). Brown faced a strong challenge from Republican Sharon Kennedy in 2012 and lost the election.
5. Because in-text citations of unsigned newspaper articles and campaign advertisements and some citations of campaign spending reports are awkward and we rely heavily on such sources in this chapter, citations for these sources will be given in footnotes.
6. Data on sources of contributions to candidates come from the website followthemoney.org, which provides information for supreme court contests beginning in 1992. The proportion of campaign contributions included in the "uncoded" category is higher in earlier years than later, making it more difficult to determine the precise contributions by various industries in the 1990s and to compare contribution sources across years.
7. Barber attributes some of that success to Ohio's use of nonpartisan ballots in supreme court elections. Some scholars (e.g., Lee 1960; Hawley 1973) argue that the nonpartisan ballot favors Republican candidates (but see Schaffner, Streb, and Wright 2007, for a competing argument).
8. Brown went on to win more than 60 percent of the vote.
9. State ex rel. Carter v. Celebrezze, 63 Ohio St. 2d 326 (1980).
10. Krupansky was appointed to the bench when Justice Paul Brown resigned.
11. "Television Ad Hit Abilities of Celebrezze," *Columbus Dispatch,* September 25, 1984, D4.
12. Columbus & Southern Ohio Electric Company v. Public Utilities Commission of Ohio, 10 Ohio St. 3d 12 (1984).
13. Corrigan lost to Republican Andrew Douglas, who received the endorsement of the Council of the American Federation of State, County, and Municipal Employees. As we will see, even with his Republican partisan affiliation Douglas became a favorite of labor because of his voting record once on the court.
14. "Celebrezze Takes Blame for His Brother's Election Loss," *Columbus Dispatch,* November 9, 1985, D5.

15. To illustrate the difference in focus by interest groups regarding the other two supreme court races on the ballot, labor contributed $53,000 and $20,000 respectively to the two Democratic candidates.
16. Ironically, after this victory for the business community, business groups were the primary source of funding for the 1987 initiative to replace elections for Ohio's appellate courts with the Missouri Plan, while the AFL-CIO funded the campaign against this proposal. The ballot measure lost by a 2-1 margin (Felice and Kilwein 1992).
17. In 1991, Justices Andrew Douglas and Craig Wright got into a physical altercation in Justice Alice Robie Resnick's chambers. Moyer was criticized for not recusing himself from cases involving a lawyer with whom he had worked; Celebrezze also regularly came under attack for perceived conflicts of interest with parties who appeared before the court.
18. "1 Million Spent on Supreme Court Races," *Columbus Dispatch,* December 17, 1988, 4B.
19. City of Rocky River v. State Employment Relations Board, 39 Ohio St. 3d 196 (1988), 43 Ohio St. 3d 1 (1989).
20. DeRolph v. State, 78 Ohio St. 3d 193 (1997).
21. Followthemoney.org. Accessed October 26, 2015, at http://www.followthemoney.org/show-me?c-t-eid=13009856&d-cci=98#[{3|{1|.
22. Candidates for chief justice were limited to $500,000, while candidates for associate justice were capped at $350,000. A federal district court issued a preliminary injunction against enforcement of the caps late in the 1996 campaign. Suster v. Marshall, 951 F. Supp. 693 (N.D. Ohio 1996).
23. DeRolph v. State, 89 Ohio St. 3d 1 (2000).
24. State ex rel. Ohio Academy of Trial Lawyers v. Sheward, 86 Ohio St. 3d 451 (1999).
25. In terms of campaign contributions, the race was not particularly special.
26. A federal district court struck down the limits on spending by judicial candidates in Suster v. Marshall, 121 F. Supp. 2d 1141 (N.D. Ohio 2000), issued in late September.
27. Although Citizens for a Strong Ohio was supported by the Ohio Chamber of Commerce, the actual donors to the group were not disclosed because the group considered itself to be not a political action committee, but an issue advocacy committee. The latter was not required to file campaign finance reports. This issue was litigated for several years, until 2004, when the group was forced to make its contributors public—which it did in early 2005. Ohio Elections Commission v. Ohio Chamber of Commerce, 158 Ohio App. 3d 557 (10th Dist. 2004); appeal dismissed in Ohio Elections Commission v. Ohio Chamber of Commerce, 104 Ohio St. 3d 1435 (2004). Not surprisingly the contributors were primarily business, banks, and insurance companies, including Procter and Gamble, Fifth Third Bank, and Ohio Farmers Insurance.
28. The commission ultimately ruled that the anti-Resnick ad was false (Nash 2005).
29. Like Citizens for a Strong Ohio two years earlier, Informed Citizens of Ohio refused to disclose their contributors.
30. Informed Citizens of Ohio, "Stratton Lawsuits." Accessed October 26, 2015, at http://www.brennancenter.org/sites/default/files/analysis/Buying_Time/OH_ICO_Stratton_Endorsement.pdf.

31. Citizens for an Independent Court, "On Our Side." Accessed October 26, 2015, at http://www.brennancenter.org/sites/default/files/analysis/Buying_Time/OH_CFIC_Black_%26_Burnside_On_Our_Side.pdf.
32. "Two Sides" was not the only ad condemned by the Ohio State Bar Association. Altogether, the organization criticized five television ads funded by issue-advocacy groups as "impugn[ing] the integrity of the court" (Craig 2002c).
33. Citizens for an Independent Court, "Black and Burnside 15." Accessed October 26, 2015, at http://www.brennancenter.org/sites/default/files/analysis/Buying_Time/OH_CFIC_Black_%26_Burnside_15.pdf.
34. Westfield Insurance Company v. Galatis, 100 Ohio St. 3d 216 (2003).
35. Scott-Pontzer v. Liberty Mutual Fire Insurance Company, 85 Ohio St. 3d 660 (1999).
36. This monetary advantage has not always guaranteed victory. In 2012, William O'Neill beat Justice Robert Cupp despite spending essentially no money. The race is clearly an outlier. O'Neill had run for the supreme court before and lost, but he received press coverage for his unwillingness to raise significant sums of money. He received similar coverage in 2012. It also seems likely that his Irish last name in a state with a long history of support for Irish candidates helped him a great deal in a low-information contest.
37. Four seats were up for election because Justice Cook received a federal judgeship. Governor Taft appointed Terrence O'Donnell to replace Cook. O'Donnell then had to run to complete the remainder of Cook's term.
38. Because of Justice Pfeifer, Republicans still would have maintained a majority.
39. Of course, as we will see, that candidate (William O'Neill) would later go on to victory using the same strategy regarding campaign contributions.
40. William O'Neill once again refused to seek donations because of his concern that campaign contributions corrupted the courts.
41. The decision was Dicenzo v. A-Best Products Company, 120 Ohio St. 3d 149 (2008).
42. Partnership for Ohio's Future, "Team You Can Trust." Accessed October 26, 2015, at http://www.brennancenter.org/sites/default/files/legacy/Buying%20Time%202010/STSUPCT_OH_PFOF_TEAM_YOU_CAN_TRUST.pdf.
43. Followthemoney.org. Accessed October 26, 2015, at http://www.followthemoney.org/show-me?f-eid=6469956&y=2012.
44. Ohio Republican Party, "When Crime Occurs 2." Accessed October 26, 2015, at http://www.brennancenter.org/sites/default/files/analysis/STSUPCT_OH_OHRP_WHEN_CRIME_OCCURS_REV.pdf.
45. Partnership for Ohio's Future, "Raised." Accessed October 26, 2015, at http://www.brennancenter.org/sites/default/files/analysis/Buying_Time/STSUPCT_OH_PFOF_CUPP_RAISED.PDF.

THREE Voters' Response to Electoral Campaigns

1. In some years, subsets of respondents were given information on the candidates beyond the names that are the sole information provided on Ohio's ballot for judicial candidates, in order to test the impact of that information on participation and choice. Those respondents are not included in the analyses in this chapter, except for one brief comparison of voters who were told the candidates' party affiliations and others who were not given that information

2. Some states include information about incumbency, occupation, and city of residence on the ballot. Two studies found evidence that incumbency and occupation designations affected voting in California elections (Dubois 1984; McDermott 2005), but a survey experiment in the context of Ohio Supreme Court elections found little effect for these designations or for city of residence (Klein and Baum 2001, 716–18).
3. On the impact of partisan and nonpartisan ballots on voting in nonjudicial contests, see Schaffner, Streb, and Wright (2001) and Schaffner and Streb (2002). Survey experiments in Ohio and North Carolina indicated that levels of partisan voting were far higher when candidates' party affiliations were provided (Klein and Baum 2001; Burnett and Tiede 2015; see also Squire and Smith 1988). The same is true of multiyear and multistate analyses of county-level correlations between voting for supreme court justice and for president and governor (Dubois 1980, chaps. 3 and 6; Kritzer 2015, chap. 6). However, one study based on multistate surveys of voters produced mixed results, with significantly greater partisan voting under partisan ballots in 2012 but not in 2010 (Bonneau and Cann 2015).
4. This figure was estimated from data in Barber (1982, 35).
5. This figure does not include a contest in 1950 to fill a vacancy in which the two leading candidates were both Republicans.
6. J. Ross Haffey, a Democrat, ran as an independent candidate in 1990 and 1992. Haffey received significant shares of the vote, 10 percent in 1990 and 9 percent in 1992. His presence on the ballot may have swung one or both of those elections to the Republican candidates. We do not include Haffey voters in this model or in the models that we present later in this section.

   Although the terms *pro-business* and *pro-plaintiff* are something of an oversimplification, we use those terms to refer to the candidate supported by the business community and the opposing candidate.
7. As discussed in chapter 2, groups' independent spending on television air time in supreme court contests has been compiled by state for most election years between 2000 and 2014 and for specific contests in some of those years in a series of reports entitled *The New Politics of Judicial Elections,* presented by the Justice at Stake Campaign and its affiliated groups. By far the largest sum was found in the Resnick-O'Donnell contest in 2000.

   Of the years for which the *New Politics* reports provide data for individual commercials, pro-business candidates had an enormous advantage in independent spending on commercials in 2004, substantial advantages in 2000 and 2008, and a small disadvantage in 2002.
8. We use the natural log of the spending figures for the multivariate analyses in this chapter, on the assumption that the incremental effect of additional spending declines as the overall level of spending increases. If the difference between the two logged spending amounts is substituted for the difference in actual spending, the correlation declines to .295.

   To a degree, of course, monetary contributions to candidates reflect expectations about candidates' prospects for success. Thus, the causality between spending and vote shares runs in both directions. But voters in supreme court contests typically start out with only limited information on the candidates, so the competing campaigns are responsible for a high proportion of the information that voters have when they go to the polls. In turn, the relative size of the two campaigns—whatever its sources—can have a powerful impact on voters' choices.

9. We have some evidence of the impact of candidates' spending on name recognition. In the seven Ohio Supreme Court contests between 1986 and 1990, survey respondents were asked to give their ratings of the two candidates on a standard "feeling thermometer," with a range of 0 to 100. Not surprisingly, many respondents did not know enough about a candidate to offer a rating, and many others offered a neutral rating of 50. For the seven contests, we calculated differences between the Democratic and Republican candidates in spending, in the proportion of voters offering a rating, and in the proportion of voters offering a rating other than 50. Using the differences as variables, the contest-level correlation between spending differences and differences in the proportions of voters who could rate the candidates was .899, and the correlation between spending and non-50 ratings was .946. Chief Justice Frank Celebrezze came to the 1986 campaign with pre-established name recognition, but the correlations were about the same when the Celebrezze-Moyer contest was removed.
10. There is an interesting discussion of potential influences on the outcomes of Ohio judicial elections in Mallory v. State of Ohio, 38 F. Supp. 2d 525, 534–37 (S. D. Ohio 1997).
11. Besides the two Celebrezzes who served on the Ohio Supreme Court, other Celebrezzes were active in politics before and during the 1980s, including Anthony Celebrezze (who served as mayor of Cleveland, as a cabinet member in the Kennedy and Johnson administrations, and as a federal appellate judge) and Anthony Celebrezze Jr. (who served as Ohio secretary of state and attorney general). Browns have been abundant in Ohio politics. In 1966 Browns ran in the general election for five statewide offices, including both supreme court seats, and in both 1972 and 1978 three of the four candidates for associate justice in the general election were Browns (see Dubois 1980, 84; Suddes 2002, 45–46). The prominence of Browns has faded over time, but in 2015 there were five judges named Brown or Browne in Franklin County (Columbus) (Futty 2015), and one of Ohio's U.S. senators is Sherrod Brown.

    Sweeney may belong in the category of familiar names as well because of the number of candidates for statewide office with that name (Lopeman 1999, 80n22). However, Sweeney is covered in the Irish name variable that we discuss next.
12. Irish names have positive connotations in judicial contests in at least one other place (Klumpp 2011).
13. These means do not include 1994; the survey items from which participation levels were calculated in 1994 were not fully comparable with those for the other years. One study (Adamany and Dubois 1980) identified survey respondents who appeared to be "forgetful" voters in a supreme court contest and found that they were less educated, less interested in politics, and less knowledgeable about politics than those who remembered that they had participated in that contest.
14. However, in the five election years in which the survey asked interviewers to assess respondents' information levels, there was a consistently strong relationship between lower information levels and roll-off when that variable was added to the equations. This was not true of political knowledge, as measured by the number of items answered correctly, in the three years in which knowledge items were in-

cluded. This finding may be an artifact of the high frequency of refusal to respond to knowledge items.

15. In the analysis of vote shares shown in table 3.1, we included only the name Brown as a potential advantage for a candidate, because Celebrezze had mixed connotations. In this analysis we include Celebrezze along with Brown, since either positive or negative reactions to the name Celebrezze could spur voter participation.
16. These results somewhat understate the overall effect of campaign spending. If we substitute combined spending by the two sides for the separate spending variables and compare the median amount with the median for the four highest-spending contests, the difference is 3.85 percent.
17. If the O'Neill-O'Donnell 2006 contest is excluded because of O'Neill's very low spending figure, the correlation becomes slightly negative (-.056).
18. We combined the weak identifier and leaner categories because of the ambiguity about how they should be ordered on the scale that goes from strong identifiers to independents (Weisberg 1983, 373–74).
19. In the 1984 and 1986 surveys, there were only three categories, which we coded as 1, 3, and 5. In some later surveys there were seven categories, which we collapsed to five by combining those who were "extremely" and "somewhat" liberal or conservative.
20. The technique was xtmelogit, as implemented in Stata. The unit of analysis at the individual level was the voter in a particular contest; thus, a voter who participated in more than one supreme court contest in an election year was counted for multiple units of analysis.
21. Only a portion of the surveys included variables to measure respondents' income directly, so that variable is not included in the regression model.
22. We use the CLARIFY procedure developed by Tomz, Wittenberg, and King (2003).
23. Overall, independents with no leaning toward either party did not consistently favor candidates from one party or the other. But the small numbers of supreme court voters who were pure independents in some of the survey years caution against inferring a great deal from this pattern.
24. The decision was The State ex rel. Ohio Academy of Trial Lawyers v. Sheward, 86 Ohio St. 3d 451 (1999).
25. We leave Brown aside because he did not run for a second term.
26. The classic statement of the difficulty of providing accurate reasons for choices is Nisbett and Wilson (1977). A response by Smith and Miller (1978) took a more positive view of people's accuracy about their reasons. The evidence for "on-line processing" of information about candidates provides good reason to expect quite imperfect recall of bases for choice (Lodge, Steenbergen, and Brau 1995).
27. The proportion of possibly policy-related reasons was very similar in the less visible John E. Corrigan-Douglas contest.
28. The reasons offered by voters in this contest and in the associate justice contests in 1986 and 1988 are discussed in greater detail in Hojnacki and Baum (1992a).
29. As an experimental manipulation, some respondents were given the party affiliations of the candidates. As would be expected, the effect of knowledge about the candidates on party-line voting was weaker among those respondents.

30. That estimate is based on multiplying the proportion of voters who were Republicans by the proportion who knew the candidates' ideological positions and then by the proportionate difference in votes between the knowledgeable Republicans and other Republicans, and then doing the same for Democrats.
31. If the two contests in which Douglas and Pfeifer initially ran for the supreme court are included, the relationship for this variable is significant at a .090 level in a two-tailed test—a weaker but still meaningful relationship.
32. In light of the findings for this variable, we might expect the 1998 contest in which the Democratic candidate actually ran to the right of Pfeifer to have an especially low correlation. But that correlation was at about the same level as that for one of Douglas's contests and was substantially higher than the correlation for the other Douglas contest.
33. This discussion of a possible Republican advantage in nonpartisan elections is based primarily on Schaffner, Streb, and Wright (2007, 240–42).
34. This conclusion follows from the fact that in the survey years, the mean share of the vote for Republican supreme court candidates was only 1.6 percent higher than the mean for Republican candidates at the top of the ticket, compared with 5.3 percent for the other election years.
35. Two appointed Democratic incumbents ran in subsequent elections; both were defeated.

FOUR Findings and Implications

1. This is not to say there have been no changes at all (see Schotland 1985; Champagne 2001a, 1403).
2. One noteworthy exception, discussed in chapter 2, was a 2012 television commercial by the state Republican Party that attacked Democratic candidate William O'Neill for alleged sympathy toward a rapist in a court of appeals opinion. One study found that in 1985, the justices who were strongly pro-plaintiff in tort cases had highly pro-prosecution voting records in criminal cases (Leonard 1989, 973; see also Lopeman 1999, 74–75).
3. Examples include Minnesota (see Olson 2010) and California (see Mintz 2010).

REFERENCES

Abramowitz, Alan I., and Jeffrey A. Segal. 1992. *Senate Elections.* Ann Arbor: University of Michigan Press.

Adamany, David, and Philip Dubois. 1975. "The 'Forgetful' Voter and an Underreported Vote." *Public Opinion Quarterly* 39: 227–31.

Adamany, David, and Mack C. Shelley II. 1980. "Encore! The Forgetful Voter." *Public Opinion Quarterly* 44: 234–40.

American Judicature Society. 2011. *Judicial Merit Selection: Current Status.* Des Moines, IA: American Judicature Society.

Aumann, Francis R. 1931. "The Selection, Tenure, Retirement and Compensation of Judges in Ohio." *University of Cincinnati Law Review* 5: 408–28.

Bannon, Alicia, Eric Velasco, and Linda Casey. 2013. *The New Politics of Judicial Elections 2011–12.* Washington, DC: Justice at Stake.

Barber, Kathleen L. 1971. "Ohio Judicial Elections—Nonpartisan Premises with Partisan Results." *Ohio State Law Journal* 32: 762–89.

———. 1972. "Selection of Ohio Appellate Judges: A Case Study in Invisible Politics." In *Political Behavior and Public Issues in Ohio,* edited by John J. Gargan and James G. Coke, 175–230. Kent, OH: Kent State University Press.

———. 1982. "Nonpartisan Ballots and Voter Confusion in Judicial Elections." Paper presented at annual meeting of the Midwest Political Science Association, Milwaukee, April–May.

———. 1984. "Judicial Politics in Ohio." In *Government and Politics in Ohio,* edited by Carl Lieberman, 89–133. Lanham, MD: University Press of America.

Barkdull, Howard L. 1939. "Analysis of Ohio Vote on Appointive Judiciary." *Journal of the American Judicature Society* 22: 197–98.

Barnes, Clifton. 2005. "Tort Reform Momentum Slowed but Not Stopped." *Bar Leader* 29 (July–August): 6–8.

Bartels, Larry M. 1993. "Messages Received: The Political Impact of Media Exposure." *American Political Science Review* 87: 267–85.

Baum, Lawrence. 1987. "Explaining the Vote in Judicial Elections: The 1984 Ohio Supreme Court Elections." *Western Political Quarterly* 40: 361–71.

———. 1988–89. "Voters' Information in Judicial Elections: The 1986 Contests for the Ohio Supreme Court." *Kentucky Law Journal* 77: 645–70.

———. 2012. *American Courts: Process and Policy.* 7th ed. Boston: Wadsworth.

Baum, Lawrence, Thomas R. Gray, and David Klein. 2017. "Measuring the Impact of Election Outcomes on Voting in State Supreme Courts." In *Judicial Elections in the 21st Century,* edited by Chris W. Bonneau and Melinda Gann Hall. New York: Routledge.

Baum, Lawrence, and David Klein. 2007. "Voter Responses to High-Visibility Judicial Campaigns." In *Running for Judge: The Rising Political, Financial, and Legal Stakes of Judicial Elections,* edited by Matthew J. Streb, 140–64. New York: New York University Press.

Bayne, William C. 2000. "Lynchard's Candidacy: Ads Putting Spice into Justice Race." *Memphis Commercial Appeal,* October 29, 2000, DS1.

Berkson, Larry C. 1980. *Judicial Selection in the United States: A Compendium of Provisions.* Chicago: American Judicature Society.

Bernhard, William, and Brian R. Sala. 2006. "The Remaking of an American Senate: The 17th Amendment and Ideological Responsiveness." *Journal of Politics* 68: 345–57.

Bonneau, Chris W. 2005. "Electoral Verdicts: Incumbent Defeats in State Supreme Court Elections." *American Politics Research* 33: 818–41.

———. 2006. "Vacancies on the Bench: Open-Seat Elections for State Supreme Courts." *Justice System Journal* 27: 143–59.

Bonneau, Chris W., and Damon M. Cann. 2015. *Voters' Verdicts: Citizens, Campaigns, and Institutions in State Supreme Court Elections.* Charlottesville: University of Virginia Press.

Bonneau, Chris W., and Melinda Gann Hall. 2009. *In Defense of Judicial Elections.* New York: Routledge.

Bonneau, Chris W., Melinda Gann Hall, and Matthew J. Streb. 2011. "White Noise: The Unrealized Effects of *Republican Party of Minnesota v. White* on Judicial Elections." *Justice System Journal* 32: 247–68.

Brace, Paul, and Brent D. Boyea. 2007. "Judicial Selection Methods and Capital Punishment in the American States." In *Running for Judge: The Rising Political, Financial, and Legal Stakes of Judicial Elections,* 186–203. New York: New York University Press.

———. 2008. "State Public Opinion, the Death Penalty, and the Practice of Electing Judges." *American Journal of Political Science* 52: 360–72.

Bradshaw, James. 1996a. "Republican Justices Finish First—and Last—in Ratings by Chamber." *Columbus Dispatch,* January 24, 2B.

———. 1996b. "Casino Backers, Opponents Bet $9.6 Million on November Vote." *Columbus Dispatch,* December 14, 4C.

———. 2000. "High Court Unchanged Despite Negative TV Ads." *Columbus Dispatch,* November 8, 1A.

Burnett, Craig M., and Lydia Tiede. 2015. "Party Labels and Vote Choice in Judicial Elections." *American Politics Research* 43: 232–54.

Byrne, Gary C., and J. Kristian Pueschel. 1974. "But Who Should I Vote for for County Coroner?" *Journal of Politics* 36: 778–84.

Caldarone, Richard P., Brandice Canes-Wrone, and Tom S. Clark. 2009. "Partisan Labels and Democratic Accountability: An Analysis of State Supreme Court Abortion Decisions." *Journal of Politics* 71: 560–73.

Caldeira, Gregory A., and John R. Wright. 1995. "Lobbying for Justice: The Rise of Organized Conflict in the Politics of Federal Judgeships." In *Contemplating Courts,* edited by Lee Epstein, 44–71. Washington, DC: CQ Press.

Candisky, Catherine. 2012. "Tight Supreme Court Race." *Columbus Dispatch,* October 25, 3B.

Canes-Wrone, Brandice, Tom S. Clark, and Jason P. Kelly. 2014. "Judicial Selection and Death Penalty Decisions." *American Political Science Review* 108: 23–39.

Cann, Damon M. 2007. "Justice for Sale? Campaign Contributions and Judicial Decisionmaking." *State Politics & Policy Quarterly* 7: 281–97.

Canon, Bradley C., and Lawrence Baum. 1981. "Patterns of Adoption of Tort Law Innovations: An Application of Diffusion Theory to Judicial Doctrines." *American Political Science Review* 75: 975–87.

Caufield, Rachel P. 2007. "The Changing Tone of Judicial Election Campaigns as a Result of *White.*" In *Running for Judge: The Rising Political, Financial, and Legal Stakes of Judicial Elections,* edited by Matthew J. Streb, 34–58. New York: New York University Press.

Celebrezze, Frank D. 1982. "Ohioans Gain Rights: The Supreme Court of Ohio." *Ohio Northern University Law Review* 9: 559–62.

———. 1983. "The Supreme Court of Ohio: 1982–83 Term." *Ohio Northern University Law Review* 10: 675–79.

Champagne, Anthony. 2001a. "Interest Groups and Judicial Elections." *Loyola of Los Angeles Law Review* 34: 1391–409.

———. 2001b. "Political Parties and Judicial Elections." *Loyola of Los Angeles Law Review* 34: 1411–27.

Cheek, Kyle, and Anthony Champagne. 2005. *Judicial Politics in Texas: Partisanship, Money, and Politics in State Courts.* New York: Peter Lang.

Clubb, Jerome M., and Michael W. Traugott. 1972. "National Patterns of Referenda Voting: The 1968 Election." In *People and Politics in Urban Society,* edited by Harlan Hahn, 137–69. Beverly Hills, CA: SAGE Publications.

Corriher, Billy. 2012. "Partisan Judicial Elections and the Distorting Influence of Campaign Cash." Washington, DC: Center for American Progress.

Craig, Jon. 2002a. "Supreme Court Candidates Profess Their Impartiality." *Columbus Dispatch,* September 8, 1C.

———. 2002b. "Stratton Picks Up Campaign Cash from Doctors." *Columbus Dispatch,* October 25, 9B.

———. 2002c. "Republicans Retain 5-2 Majority with Dual Victory." *Columbus Dispatch,* November 6, 1A.

———. 2003. "GOP Justices Out-Raised Democratic Contenders." *Columbus Dispatch,* March 4, 3D.

———. 2004. "Republicans Split $9 Million." *Columbus Dispatch,* October 29, 1B.

Curtin, Michael. 1986. "Scales Collapsing Again." *Columbus Dispatch,* October 28, 4D.

———. 1988. "AFL-CIO to Focus on Putting Democrats in State's Top Court." *Columbus Dispatch,* June 9, 3C.

Dubois, Philip L. 1980. *From Ballot to Bench: Judicial Elections and the Quest for Accountability.* Austin: University of Texas Press.

———. 1984. "Voting Cues in Nonpartisan Trial Court Elections: A Multivariate Assessment." *Law & Society Review* 18: 395–436.

Felice, John D., and John C. Kilwein. 1992. "Strike One, Strike Two . . .: The History of and Prospect for Judicial Reform in Ohio." *Judicature* 75: 193–200.

Flanigan, William H., Nancy H. Zingale, Elizabeth A. Theiss-Morse, and Michael W. Wagner. 2015. *Political Behavior of the American Electorate.* 13th ed. Los Angeles: CQ Press.

Frederick, Brian, and Matthew J. Streb. 2008. "Paying the Price for a Seat on the Bench: Campaign Spending in Contested State Intermediate Appellate Court Elections." *State Politics & Policy Quarterly* 8: 410–29.

Futty, John. 2015. "When in Doubt, Just Ask Them for Judge Brown." *Columbus Dispatch,* July 23, 4B.

Gaddie, Ronald Keith, and Charles S. Bullock. 2000. *Elections to Open Seats in the U.S. House: Where the Action Is.* Lanham, MD: Rowman and Littlefield.

Geyh, Charles Gardner. 2003. "Why Judicial Elections Stink." *Ohio State Law Journal* 64: 43–79.

Gibson, James L. 2012. *Electing Judges: The Surprising Effects of Campaigning on Judicial Legitimacy.* Chicago: University of Chicago Press.

Gibson, James L., Jeffrey A. Gottfried, Michael X. Delli Carpini, and Kathleen Hall Jamieson. 2011. "The Effects of Judicial Campaign Activity on the Legitimacy of Courts: A Survey-Based Experiment." *Political Research Quarterly* 64: 545–58.

Goldberg, Deborah. 2007. "Interest Group Participation in Judicial Elections." In *Running for Judge: The Rising Political, Financial, and Legal Stakes of Judicial Elections,* edited by Matthew J. Streb, 73–95. New York: New York University Press.

Goldberg, Deborah, Craig Holman, and Samantha Sanchez. 2002. *The New Politics of Judicial Elections.* New York: Brennan Center for Justice.

Goldberg, Deborah, Sarah Samis, Edwin Bender, and Rachel Weiss. 2005. *The New Politics of Judicial Elections 2004.* Washington, DC: Justice at Stake Campaign.

Gordon, Sanford C., and Gregory A. Huber. 2007. "The Effect of Electoral Competitiveness on Incumbent Behavior." *Quarterly Journal of Political Science* 2: 107–38.

Greene, Richard. 1986. "The Hanging Judges of Business." *Forbes,* April 7, 62–64.

Greytak, Scott, Alicia Bannon, Allyse Falce, and Linda Casey. 2015. *Bankrolling the*

Bench: The New Politics of Judicial Elections 2013–14. Washington, DC: Justice at Stake.

Hall, Kermit L. 1984. "Progressive Reform and the Decline of Democratic Accountability: The Popular Election of State Supreme Court Judges, 1850–1920." *American Bar Foundation Research Journal* 1984: 345–69.

Hall, Melinda Gann. 1987. "Constituent Influence in State Supreme Courts: Conceptual Notes and a Case Study." *Journal of Politics* 49: 1117–24.

———. 1992. "Electoral Politics and Strategic Voting in State Supreme Courts." *Journal of Politics* 54: 427–46.

———. 1995. "Justices as Representatives: Elections and Judicial Politics in the American States." *American Politics Quarterly* 23: 485–503.

———. 2001. "State Supreme Courts in American Democracy: Probing the Myths of Judicial Reform." *American Political Science Review* 95: 315–30.

———. 2007. "Competition as Accountability in State Supreme Court Elections." In *Running for Judge: The Rising Political, Financial, and Legal Stakes of Judicial Elections,* edited by Matthew J. Streb, 165–85. New York: New York University Press.

———. 2015. *Attacking Judges: How Campaign Advertising Influences State Supreme Court Elections.* Stanford, CA: Stanford University Press.

Hall, Melinda Gann, and Chris W. Bonneau. 2006. "Does Quality Matter? Challengers in State Supreme Court Elections." *American Journal of Political Science* 50: 20–33.

———. 2008. "Mobilizing Interest: The Effects of Money on Citizen Participation in State Supreme Court Elections." *American Journal of Political Science* 52: 457–70.

Hallett, Joe. 1999a. "Court Ruling Lays Bare Republican Infighting." *Columbus Dispatch,* August 17, 1A.

———. 1999b. "Republicans Closing in on Choice for Supreme Court Bid." *Columbus Dispatch,* November 23, 3C.

———. 2000a. "Supreme Court Race Features Outsider Mud." *Columbus Dispatch,* June 11, 3B.

———. 2000b. "Biggest Money in Court Races Still Secret." *Columbus Dispatch,* December 16, 7B.

———. 2007. "What Went On in the Supreme Court." *Columbus Dispatch,* March 18, A1, A8, A9.

Hanssen, F. Andrew. 2004. "Learning about Judicial Independence: Institutional Change in the State Courts." *Journal of Legal Studies* 33: 431–73.

Hawley, Willis D. 1973. *Nonpartisan Elections and the Case for Party Politics.* New York: John Wiley.

Herrnson, Paul S. 2011. *Congressional Elections: Campaigning at Home and in Washington.* 6th ed. Washington, DC: CQ Press.

Hignett, Christen Spears. 2005. "Comment: Ohio's Public School Funding System: The Unanswered Questions and the Unresolved Problems of *DeRolph.*" *Capital University Law Review* 33: 739–85.

Hillygus, D. Sunshine, and Simon Jackman. 2003. "Voter Decision Making in

Election 2000: Campaign Effects, Partisan Activation, and the Clinton Legacy." *American Journal of Political Science* 47: 583–96.
Hinckley, Barbara. 1976. "Issues, Information Costs, and Congressional Elections." *American Politics Quarterly* 4: 131–52.
Hinckley, Barbara, Richard Hofstetter, and John Kessel. 1974. "Information and the Vote: A Comparative Election Study." *American Politics Quarterly* 2: 131–58.
Hogan, Robert E. 2000. "The Costs of Representation in State Legislatures: Explaining Variations in Campaign Spending." *Social Science Quarterly* 81: 941–56.
———. 2004. "Challenger Emergence, Incumbent Success, and Electoral Accountability in State Legislative Elections." *Journal of Politics* 66: 1283–303.
———. 2005. "Gubernatorial Coattail Effects in State Legislative Elections." *Political Research Quarterly* 58: 587–97.
Hojnacki, Marie, and Lawrence Baum. 1992a. "Choosing Judicial Candidates: How Voters Explain Their Decisions." *Judicature* 75: 300–309.
———. 1992b. "'New-Style' Judicial Campaigns and the Voters: Economic Issues and Union Members in Ohio." *Western Political Quarterly* 45: 921–48.
Holder, Paul. 1980. "That's Yarbrough—Spelled with One 'O': A Study of Judicial Misbehavior in Texas." In *Practicing Texas Politics,* 4th ed., edited by Eugene W. Jones, Joe E. Ericson, Lyle C. Brown, and Robert S. Trotter, Jr., 447–53. Boston: Houghton Mifflin.
Huber, Gregory A., and Sanford C. Gordon. 2004. "Accountability and Coercion: Is Justice Blind When It Runs for Office?" *American Journal of Political Science* 48: 247–63.
Jacobson, Gary C. 1989. "Strategic Politicians and the Dynamics of U.S. House Elections, 1946–86." *American Political Science Review* 83: 773–93.
———. 1999. "The Effect of the AFL-CIO's 'Voter Education' Campaign on the 1996 House Elections." *Journal of Politics* 61: 185–94.
Jacobson, Gary C., and Jamie L. Carson. 2015. *The Politics of Congressional Elections.* 9th ed. Lanham, MD: Rowman and Littlefield.
Jacobson, Gary C., and Samuel Kernell. 1983. *Strategy and Choice in Congressional Elections.* 2nd ed. New Haven, CT: Yale University Press.
Jewell, Malcolm E., and William E. Cassie. 1998. "Can the Legislative Campaign Finance System Be Reformed?" In *Campaign Finance in State Legislative Elections,* edited by Joel A. Thompson and Gary F. Moncrief, 209–32. Washington, DC: CQ Press.
Johnson, Alan. 2000. "Taft Raising Money for Anti-Resnick Fund." *Columbus Dispatch,* October 18, 1A.
Johnson, Charles A., Roger C. Schaefer, and R. Neal McKnight. 1978. "The Salience of Judicial Candidates and Elections." *Social Science Quarterly* 59: 371–78.
Kam, Cindy D. 2007. "Implicit Attitudes, Explicit Choices: When Subliminal Priming Predicts Candidate Preference." *Political Behavior* 29: 343–67.
Kam, Cindy D., and Elizabeth J. Zechmeister. 2013. "Name Recognition and Candidate Support." *American Journal of Political Science* 57: 971–86.

Kang, Michael S., and Joanna M. Shepherd. 2011. "The Partisan Price of Justice: An Empirical Analysis of Campaign Contributions and Judicial Decisions." *New York University Law Review* 86: 69–130.

Kermisch, Amos A. 1978. "Campaign Tough for the High Court." *Cleveland Plain Dealer,* October 23, 11-A.

Klein, David, and Lawrence Baum. 2001. "Ballot Information and Voting Decisions in Judicial Elections." *Political Research Quarterly* 54: 709–28

Klumpp, Albert J. 2011. "Judicial Primary Elections in Cook County, Illinois: Fear the Irish Women!" *DePaul Law Review* 60: 821–47.

Kritzer, Herbert M. 2015. *Justices on the Ballot: Continuity and Change in State Supreme Court Elections.* New York: Cambridge University Press.

Langer, Laura. 2002. *Judicial Review in State Supreme Courts.* Albany: SUNY Press.

Lee, Eugene C. 1960. *The Politics of Nonpartisanship.* Berkeley: University of California Press.

Leonard, James. 1989. "Ideology and Judicial Behavior: A Statistical Study of the Ohio Supreme Court: 1970, 1975, 1980 and 1985 Terms." *University of Cincinnati Law Review* 57: 935–86.

Lewis-Beck, Michael S., William G. Jacoby, Helmut Norpoth, and Herbert F. Weisberg. 2008. *The American Voter Revisited.* Ann Arbor: University of Michigan Press.

Liptak, Adam, and Janet Roberts. 2006. "Campaign Cash Mirrors a High Court's Rulings." *New York Times,* October 1, 1, 22–23.

Lodge, Milton, Marco R. Steenbergen, and Shawn Brau. 1995. "The Responsive Voter: Campaign Information and the Dynamics of Candidate Evaluation." *American Political Science Review* 89: 309–26.

Lopeman, Charles S. 1999. *The Activist Advocate: Policy Making in State Supreme Courts.* Westport, CT: Praeger.

Lovrich, Nicholas P., Jr., and Charles H. Sheldon. 1983. "Voters in Contested, Nonpartisan Judicial Elections: A Responsible Electorate or a Problematic Public?" *Western Political Quarterly* 36: 241–56.

Lowe, Roger K. 1986. "Incumbents Endorsed." *Columbus Dispatch,* August 16, 2B.

———. 1988. "Supreme Court Bids Fail to Stir Interest." *Columbus Dispatch,* September 11, 4C.

———. 1989. "Resnick 'a Bit More Liberal' than Predecessor." *Columbus Dispatch,* January 1, 4B.

Lowe, Roger K., and Cliff Treyens. 1986. "Chief Justice Got More Cash Linked to Mob." *Columbus Dispatch,* October 24, 1C.

Ludlow, Randy. 2015. "Chief Justice Wants Judicial-Election Changes." *Columbus Dispatch,* August 20, 8B.

May, Melissa S. 2013. "Judicial Retention Elections after 2010." *Indiana Law Review* 46: 59–86.

McCall, Madhavi M., and Michael A. McCall. 2007. "Campaign Contributions, Judicial Decisions, and the Texas Supreme Court: Assessing the Appearance of Impropriety." *Judicature* 90: 214–25.

McDermott, Monika L. 1997. "Voting Cues in Low-Information Elections:

Candidate Gender as a Social Information Variable in Contemporary United States Elections." *American Journal of Political Science* 41: 270–83.
———. 1998. "Race and Gender Cues in Low-Information Elections." *Political Research Quarterly* 51: 895–918.
———. 2005. "Candidate Occupations and Voter Information Shortcuts." *Journal of Politics* 67: 201–19.
Mintz, Howard. 2010. "Governor Defies Stereotypes, Party Labels in Shaping California Judiciary." *San Jose Mercury News,* July 24. Retrieved from http://www.mercurynews.com/2010/07/24/governor-defies-stereotypes-party-labels-in-shaping-california-judiciary/.
Mondak, Jeffrey J. 1995. "Competence, Integrity, and the Electoral Success of Congressional Incumbents." *Journal of Politics* 57: 1043–69.
Mueller, John E. 1970. "Choosing among 133 Candidates." *Public Opinion Quarterly* 34: 395–402.
Nakanishi, Masao, Lee G. Cooper, and Harold H. Kassarjian. 1974. "Voting for a Political Candidate under Conditions of Minimal Information." *Journal of Consumer Research* 1 (September): 36–43.
Nash, James. 2005. "Anti-Resnick TV Ad Ruled False." *Columbus Dispatch,* November 11, 1C.
———. 2008. "Cordray and Two Justices Far Ahead in Fundraising." *Columbus Dispatch,* October 24, 4B.
Nelson, Michael J., Rachel Paine Caufield, and Andrew D. Martin. 2013. "OH, MI: A Note on Empirical Examinations of Judicial Elections." *State Politics & Policy Quarterly* 13: 495–511.
Nelson, Michael R., Craig A. Cohen, and Mark H. Rosenberg. 2005. "*Avery v. State Farm* Reversed by Illinois Supreme Court." *The Metropolitan Corporate Counsel.* Retrieved from http://www.metrocorpcounsel.com/pdf/2005/September/09.pdf.
Nisbett, Richard E., and Timothy D. Wilson. 1977. "Telling More Than We Can Know: Verbal Reports on Mental Processes." *Psychological Review* 84: 231–59.
Obhof, Larry J. 2005. "*DeRolph v. State* and Ohio's Long Road to an Adequate Education." *Brigham Young University Education and Law Journal* 2005 (1): 83–149.
Olson, Rochelle. 2010. "No Doubt, the State's High Court Tilts Right." *Minneapolis Star Tribune,* February 28, 1B.
Reidinger, Paul. 1987. "The Politics of Judging." *ABA Journal* 73 (April): 52–58.
Rock, Emily, and Lawrence Baum. 2010. "The Impact of High-Visibility Contests for Judgeships: Partisan Voting in Nonpartisan Elections." *State Politics & Policy Quarterly* 10: 368–96.
Rosenstone, Steven J., and John Mark Hansen. 1993. *Mobilization, Participation, and Democracy in America.* New York: Macmillan.
Rowland, Darrel. 2004. "Ban on Same-Sex Marriage Popular." *Columbus Dispatch,* August 30, 1A.
Ruth, Robert. 1992. "Chief Justice, 2 More from GOP Set for Top Court." *Columbus Dispatch,* November 4, 1D.

St. Clair, Duane. 1980. "Court Races Draw Little Attention." *Columbus Dispatch,* October 12, B3.

———. 1985. "Big-Bucks Campaigns May Cost Courts Credibility." *Columbus Dispatch,* August 11, D4.

———. 1986. "Workers' Comp in Ohio: How Bad Is it?" *Columbus Dispatch,* January 5, 4H.

Sample, James, Adam Skaggs, Jonathan Blitzer, and Linda Casey. 2010. *The New Politics of Judicial Elections 2000–2009: Decade of Change.* New York: Justice at Stake Campaign.

Schaffner, Brian F., and Matthew J. Streb. 2002. "The Partisan Heuristic in Low-Information Elections." *Public Opinion Quarterly* 66: 559–81.

Schaffner, Brian F., Matthew J. Streb, and Gerald C. Wright. 2001. "Teams without Uniforms: The Nonpartisan Ballot in State and Local Elections." *Political Research Quarterly* 54: 7–30.

———. 2007. "A New Look at the Republican Advantage in Nonpartisan Elections." *Political Research Quarterly* 60: 240–49.

Schotland, Roy A. 1985. "Elective Judges' Campaign Financing: Are State Judges' Robes the Emperor's Clothes of American Democracy?" *Journal of Law & Politics* 2: 57–167.

Shaffer, Stephen D. 1982. "Voting in Four Elective Offices: A Comparative Analysis." *American Politics Quarterly* 10: 5–30.

Shepherd, Joanna M. 2009. "Money, Politics, and Impartial Justice." *Duke Law Journal* 58: 623–85.

Shortell, Christopher. 2013. "Voting in Trial Court Elections: Ballot Roll-Off in Partisan, Nonpartisan, and Retention Elections in High-Population Counties." *Justice System Journal* 34: 153–70.

Shugerman, Jed Handelsman. 2012. *The People's Courts: Pursuing Judicial Independence in America.* Cambridge, MA: Harvard University Press.

Skaggs, Adam, Maria da Silva, Linda Casey, and Charles Hall. 2011. *The New Politics of Judicial Elections 2009–10.* New York: Justice at Stake Campaign.

Smith, Eliot R., and Frederick D. Miller. 1978. "Limits on Perception of Cognitive Processes: A Reply to Nisbett and Wilson." *Psychological Bulletin* 85: 355–62.

Sniderman, Paul M., Richard A. Brody, and Philip E. Tetlock. 1991. *Reasoning and Choice: Explorations in Political Psychology.* New York: Cambridge University Press.

Solimine, Michael E., and Richard B. Saphire. 2004. "The Selection of Judges in Ohio." In *The History of Ohio Law,* edited by Michael Les Benedict and John F. Winkler, 211–37. Athens: Ohio University Press.

Squire, Peverill, and Eric R. A. N. Smith. 1988. "The Effect of Partisan Information on Voters in Nonpartisan Elections." *Journal of Politics* 50: 169–79.

Steigerwalt, Amy. 2010. *Battle over the Bench: Senators, Interest Groups, and Lower Court Confirmations.* Charlottesville: University of Virginia Press.

Stern, Seth. 2005. "West Virginia Supreme Court Election Shows Effectiveness of Interest Groups." *Judicature* 89: 38–40.

Stimson, James A., Michael B. Mackuen, and Robert S. Erikson. 1995. "Dynamic Representation." *American Political Science Review* 89: 543–65.

Stone, Walter J., L. Sandy Maisel, and Cherie Maestas. 2004. "Quality Counts: Extending the Strategic Politician Model of Incumbent Deterrence." *American Journal of Political Science* 48: 479–95.

Streb, Matthew J. 2007. "Partisan Involvement in Partisan and Nonpartisan Trial Court Elections." In *Running for Judge: The Rising Political, Financial, and Legal Stakes of Judicial Elections,* edited by Matthew J. Streb, 96–114. New York: New York University Press.

———. 2015. *Rethinking American Electoral Democracy.* 3rd ed. New York: Routledge.

Streb, Matthew J., and Brian Frederick. 2009. "Conditions for Competition in Low-Information Judicial Elections: The Case of Intermediate Appellate Courts." *Political Research Quarterly* 62: 523–37.

———. 2011. "When Money Cannot Encourage Participation: Campaign Spending and Rolloff in Low Visibility Judicial Elections." *Political Behavior* 33: 665–84.

Streb, Matthew J., Brian Frederick, and Casey LaFrance. 2007. "Contestation, Competition, and the Potential for Accountability in Intermediate Appellate Court Elections." *Judicature* 91: 70–78.

———. 2009. "Voter Rolloff in a Low-Information Context: Evidence from Intermediate Appellate Court Elections." *American Politics Research* 37: 644–69.

Streb, Matthew J., Brian Frederick, Casey LaFrance, and Kimberly Rice. 2017. "The Latest Trends in Intermediate Appellate Court Elections." In *Judicial Elections in the 21st Century,* edited by Chris W. Bonneau and Melinda Gann Hall. New York: Routledge.

Suddes, Thomas. 2002. "Knowledge Gaps in Metropolitan Ohio: Ohio Supreme Court Contests, Newspaper Editorial Pages, and the Cue-Less Reader, 1938–98." M.S. thesis, Ohio University.

Tarr, G. Alan, and Mary Cornelia Aldis Porter. 1988. *State Supreme Courts in State and Nation.* New Haven, CT: Yale University Press.

Theis, Sandy, and T. C. Brown. 2000. "U.S. Chamber Pours $1 Million into Attack on Resnick." *Cleveland Plain Dealer,* October 27, 1A.

Thomas, Martin. 1985. "Election Proximity and Senatorial Roll Call Voting." *American Journal of Political Science* 29: 96–111.

Tomz, Michael, Jason Wittenberg, and Gary King. 2003. CLARIFY: Software for Interpreting and Presenting Statistical Results. Version 2.1. Stanford University, University of Wisconsin, and Harvard University. Available at http://gking.harvard.edu/.

Van Dunk, Emily. 1997. "Challenger Quality in State Legislative Elections." *Political Research Quarterly* 50: 793–807.

Van Tine, Warren, C. J. Slanicka, Sandra Jordan, and Michael Pierce. 1998. *In the Workers' Interest: A History of the Ohio AFL-CIO, 1958–1998.* Columbus: Center for Labor Research, Ohio State University.

Waldstein, David. 2016. "A Star Who Gave the Mets a Jolt, and Not Just at the Plate." *New York Times,* January 7, B12.

Ware, Stephen J. 1999. "Money, Politics and Judicial Decisions: A Case Study of Arbitration Law in Alabama." *Journal of Law & Politics* 15: 645–86.

Wattenberg, Martin P., Ian McAllister, and Anthony Salvanto. 2000. "How Voting Is Like Taking an SAT Test: An Analysis of American Voter Rolloff." *American Politics Quarterly* 28: 234–50.

Weisberg, Herbert F. 1983. "A New Scale of Partisanship." *Political Behavior* 5: 363–76.

Wold, John T., and John H. Culver. 1987. "The Defeat of the California Justices: The Campaign, the Electorate, and the Issue of Judicial Accountability." *Judicature* 70: 348–55.

Yost, Mary. 1986. "High Court Hopeful Seeks Women's Help." *Columbus Dispatch,* October 1, 2E.

———. 1991a. "Ohio Supreme Court Justice Brown to Announce He Won't Run Again." *Columbus Dispatch,* September 13, 1A.

———. 1991b. "Justices Make Up, Shake Hands." *Columbus Dispatch,* November 16, 2D.

Zaller, John R. 1992. *The Nature and Origins of Mass Opinion.* New York: Cambridge University Press.

INDEX

The letter "t" following a page number denotes a table, white the letter "f" indicates a figure.